Lost in Transition

Lost in Transition

ETHNOGRAPHIES

OF EVERYDAY LIFE

AFTER COMMUNISM

Kristen Ghodsee

Duke University Press   Durham and London   2011

© 2011 Duke University Press

All rights reserved

Printed in the United States of America on acid-free paper ∞

Designed by Heather Hensley

Typeset in Whitman by Keystone Typesetting, Inc.

Library of Congress Cataloging-in-Publication Data appear
on the last printed page of this book.

For Scott

CONTENTS

ECHOES OFF THE IRON CURTAIN

Those who rejoice at the present-day difficulties of the Soviet
Union and who look forward to the collapse of the empire
might wish to recall that such transformations normally occur
at very great cost, and not always in a predictable fashion.
Paul Kennedy, *The Rise and Fall of the Great Powers*

A little over twenty years ago an empire imploded. The tectonic
plates of history shifted, and an entire political and economic
system collapsed into a newly formed chasm of the soon-to-be
past. That system was based on an ideological foundation so revo-
lutionary and so far reaching that almost no one who lived during
the twentieth century remained untouched by it. After 1945, in
almost every country around the world, the contours of daily life
were shaped by an escalating global conflict that brought the
Earth the closest it has ever been to violent self-destruction. In
this modern era dominated by fears of global warming and rapid
climate change, it is all too easy to forget that it was not so long
ago when schoolchildren grew up worrying about total nuclear
annihilation. Indeed, I spent most of my own teenage years ob-
sessed with what seemed to be the inevitability of mutually assured destruction.

It all started humbly enough, with some ideas about where

profits come from, how class conflict has apparently shaped human history, and how humans are progressing toward more and more social justice. In 1848 two men, Karl Marx and Friedrich Engels, published a short pamphlet called *The Communist Manifesto*. By the end of that year there were uprisings across Europe. These early revolutions were brutally crushed, but the specter of communism haunted Europe and laid the groundwork for the Russian Revolution of 1917. Vladimir Lenin would come to power in Russia and create the Union of Soviet Socialist Republics (USSR), the world's first officially communist country. In 1919 Lenin formed the Communist International (Comintern), an organization dedicated to the violent overthrow of the international bourgeoisie. From the very beginning the West feared communist ideology and its relentless attacks on private property and free markets; the Great Depression in the Western countries allowed the Soviets to develop their planned economy and attain superpower status in just a few short decades. From a backward feudal empire of peasants, Russia emerged as an industrial giant by the 1940s. It used its power and resources to influence workers and peasants across the world to join the international revolution. And for a while it looked like the Russians just might win.

The communist message gained incredible momentum through the first half of the twentieth century (see the timeline in appendix A). After Russia, Mongolia became the second communist country in 1921. China added one billion people (or about one-fourth of the world's population) to the communist camp when Mao Zedong established the People's Republic of China in 1949. Albania, Yugoslavia, Bulgaria, Romania, Hungary, Czechoslovakia, and Poland all became communist countries after World War II. Germany was divided and the eastern part became the German Democratic Republic (GDR). Only massive Western intervention prevented Greece and Turkey from joining the communist world as well. Then it was Southeast Asia: North Korea, Vietnam, Laos, Cambodia, Indonesia, and the Philippines. Communist insurgents suddenly seemed to be everywhere. Although the United States was able to hold the North Koreans to the thirty-eighth parallel, it would suffer a humiliating defeat in Vietnam.

The Middle East also started to "turn red." South Yemen became a communist country. Egypt, Syria, and Iraq all became Soviet allies, with the leader of Egypt nationalizing the Suez Canal. Only Western intervention in Iran prevented leftist nationalization of the oil industry. As communist influence spread, Western financial interests were seriously threatened and transnational corporations were in constant fear of expropriation. In 1959 the revolution in Cuba (just ninety miles from Florida) brought the communist threat closer than it had ever been to the United States, and the Cuban Missile Crisis in 1962 would bring the world close to the brink of total nuclear destruction for the first time.

Many countries in Latin America and Africa were constantly fighting communist insurgencies as well. In 1970, the year that I was born, Chile would democratically elect a Socialist leader, leaving the United States no choice but to support a coup d'état and install a brutal military dictator to protect the rights of property owners. Nicaragua would become a communist country in 1979. In Africa, Angola, Tanzania, and Ethiopia would all have leftist revolutions. The Soviets would invade Afghanistan to support a local Communist government, and more and more nations would look to the USSR for political and economic aid. At its height, the communist ideology nominally controlled the lives and worldviews about a third of the Earth's population. As I grew up during the 1970s and 1980s, it seemed to me that the West was on the losing side of the ideological battle. I believed that the Soviets would eventually make good on their promise to bury the capitalist system. And then one day it just collapsed. In one cataclysmic convulsion of geopolitics the threat of world domination by the Soviet Union disappeared almost overnight. I was nineteen when the Berlin Wall fell and only twenty-one when the Soviet Union finally imploded in 1991. These events were sudden and had a profound impact on the generation of young people that had been raised with the idea that the Cold War would most likely end with a nuclear holocaust.

It seems incredible that only two decades later the rapid rise of communism and its spectacular fall would be almost completely forgotten. But collective forgetting is exactly what we have done, particularly among those born after 1989. In 2004 I hired a student research assistant to read through about seven hundred pages of congressional testimony titled the "Theory and Practice of Communism" from the 1970s. When she finished I asked her if she had learned anything interesting. She replied, "I learned that the KGB was actually a real thing. I just thought it was something they made up for [the TV show] *Alias*." When I recently asked a class of bright young college students to define *communism*, one raised his hand and explained it as "the political system of ancient Russia." I later inquired, "Why was the Cold War considered *cold*?" The students sat sheepishly. "What does it mean to have a *cold* war?" I pressed. A hand went up tentatively. A young woman guessed, "Is it a war you fight in Siberia?"

As someone who has spent her entire adult life studying the social effects of the collapse of communism on the men and women who lived in the former Eastern Bloc, episodes like these often leave me incredulous. The events of 1989 cut loose the familiar mooring to which I had firmly lashed the cords of my entire worldview. Everything I knew and understood about the present and the future unexpectedly shifted. I could only begin to imagine what the fall of the Berlin Wall had been like for those who lived through it. As an ethnographer of the postsocialist era, my goal is to try to see the transition through the eyes of those who weathered the chaos of the changes. Rather than relying on nationally representative survey results or quick tours of the region to interview a handful of English-speaking elites, I have done over thirteen years of sustained research on one culture where I lived for over three years, learning the language and sharing daily life with the men and women that most social science research tends to ignore. I published two academic books on the transformation of communism (*The Red Riviera* with Duke University Press in 2005 and *Muslim Lives in Eastern Europe* with Princeton University Press in 2009), both of which discussed larger economic and political issues through the stories of ordinary people. The books concerned themselves with the social theory of transition and how the end of communism differentially impacted men and women. They were the kinds of books I needed to write to engage with the scholarship in my field, to get an academic job, and become a tenured college professor.

Unlike my first two books, where the stories of daily life were always secondary to the larger theoretical arguments, I wanted to write a book that put the lives of individual men and women first. This book is a collection of essays and short stories about communism and its aftermath told from the perspective of everyday life. The majority are written in the first person, taken directly from my field notes, journal entries, and my memories of conversations or episodes that occurred in the twenty years between 1989 and 2009. All of the ethnographic pieces are based on real events that occurred while I was living and traveling in Eastern Europe, although I have changed all of the names and some of the identifying details of individual people to protect their identities. Furthermore, despite their origins in real events, it is important to remember that these chapters are filtered through my own recollections of how things happened and are inevitably told from my point of view. As much as I have tried to present the perspectives of the men and women living through these changes, it is always me doing the observing and retelling—an omnipresent Western interlocutor. As a result of this, some of the chapters focus on my own experiences as I tried to navigate the ever-unpredictable realities of living in a postsocialist country, from being stuck in a train compartment with smugglers from Istanbul to Belgrade in 1990 to surviving a day of mysterious explosions in Sofia in 2008.

The chapters in this book are unified by their focus on everyday life after communism in Eastern Europe, but they span a period of twenty years and touch on a wide variety of themes. They are ethnographic snapshots of the circumstances of individual men and women as they struggled to work their way through the postsocialist period, mere moments in a time now past. Put together, they tell a story of human resilience in the face of adversity, but they are also important on their own. The anthropologist John Borneman has argued in his *Syrian Episodes* that more than just fitting in to a broader analytical narrative about a particular place and time, ethnographic writing can also have a purely "documentary function" as well, providing basic data for future analysis. Borneman is an advocate of the *episode*, ethnographic snapshots of cultural contact between observer and observed, which can give us insights into different worldviews without having to make specific arguments about how or why those worldviews are important. I love the idea of documentary ethnography, and I like to think of this book as raw footage, shot through the lens of my perception, lightly edited through the workshop of my memory, and then pieced together on film without a script to guide the plot.

Taken together, I hope to create a picture of the quotidian, to capture what life was like for people living through the aftermath of 1989, and why it is that so many people look back with fondness on what seems to us in the West as an oppressive totalitarian era. Indeed, a series of public opinion polls taken in 2009 showed widespread nostalgia for the socialist era across East Europe, with many people believing that a strong economy is more important than a good democracy. Understanding the way ordinary people experienced both the opportunities and disappointments associated with the coming of democracy can shed light on the growing sense that something very important was lost with the passing of the communist era.

In order to explore these themes in greater depth, I have also included four short stories written in the third person (to distinguish them from the first-person ethnographic chapters). These stories are also based on my fieldwork and personal experiences, emerging out of a complex understanding of the cultural nuances of everyday life after the end of communism. This work is an attempt to bring alive the joys and sufferings of ordinary people who, from our perspective in the West, were on the losing side of the Cold War. I want to make it clear that this is not a book meant for my scholarly peers. It is a book intended for students and nonspecialists, a mere introduction to what is admittedly a very complicated history. Some of my academic colleagues will no doubt balk at the breeziness with which I handle the theoretical intricacies of various topics. But my prime directive is to write an accessible text, even if this means exorcizing most of the footnotes. I want the individual essays and short stories to speak for themselves.

My hope is that the reader will walk a hundred or so pages in someone else's postcommunist shoes. Just as people can get lulled into thinking that history is unchanging, so too we can find ourselves convinced that there are facts about culture and religion that mechanistically determine who we are and what we believe. The word *communism* has such a negative connotation to so many Western ears that people are incredulous when they hear about the growing nostalgia for it emerging throughout the former Eastern Bloc, what the Germans call *Ostalgie*. When the Western press reports that there are Russian villages resurrecting their statues of Stalin, the people there are assumed to be irrational or deluded. Why, we ask, would anyone want to bring back such an oppressive and unsustainable system? When we hear about the increasing centralized authority of Vladimir Putin, students are quick to argue that Russians might have a collective proclivity toward authoritarianism. Even my scholarly colleagues in political science are quick to denounce every antidemocratic maneuver attempted by a postsocialist government without really thinking about why people might accept more state interference in their lives after twenty years of political instability and social upheaval.

It is only by examining everyday life that we can understand that even in a time of great oppression, state violence, or radical social change, most people still wake up in the morning, get dressed, wash their clothes, eat, drink, fall in love, have babies, and grow old. It is good to remember that while people may vote only once a year, they eat three times a day. Communist travel restrictions were almost universally despised, but family vacations abroad may quickly become meaningless if there are no jobs to take a vacation from. Life doesn't stop when the world turns upside down. Generations can be proverbially lost, but the mundane rhythm of daily life always continues on.

This is not a defense of twentieth-century totalitarianism. It is an attempt to make sense of what twentieth-century totalitarianism meant to the people that lived through it and how its sudden disappearance upended individual lives, including my own. For most of us in the West, these changes meant no more than having a new set of bad guys in the James Bond movies, but the collapse of communism had exponentially more profound effects in the region. Certainly there were winners, but there were many losers, men and women who are both the victims and heroes of one of the most dramatic historical upheavals in the last century.

This book is about sharing the experiences of those everyday men and women as they eat, sleep, learn, work, love, and dream of a better world. Yes, capitalism won. Yes, twentieth-century totalitarian communism is gone, and the world is probably better off for that. But its reverberations on individual people's lives will be with us for years to come. It is essential that we understand the intimate legacies of the end of the Cold War if only so that we appreciate the social implications of such a radical geopolitical change in so short a period of time. After all, next time it could be us.

ACKNOWLEDGMENTS

Writing the acknowledgments for any book project is often more difficult than writing the book itself—there are so many people to thank. Although writing can be a solitary and lonely pastime, family members, friends, colleagues, and eager students have always been there to help and support me in a multiplicity of ways. Additionally, there are the many friends, acquaintances, and strangers in Bulgaria and throughout Eastern Europe who shared their stories with me and inspired me to write about everyday life. My deepest thanks goes out to all who assisted me with this project but especially to Maxime Billick, Jim Clark, Anne Clifford, Vera Dellwig, Christian Filipov, Josephine Gussa, Laura Henry, Page Herrlinger, Doug Rogers, Scott Sehon, and Jennifer Scanlon who all read and commented on early portions of the manuscript. A special acknowledgment goes out to Anelia Atanassova for coming up with the title.

I would also like to thank the American Anthropological Association and the journal *Anthropology of East Europe Review*, who previously published earlier versions of "Basset Hounds in the Balkans" and "Shopaholic in Eastern Europe." Earlier, shortened portions of "Basset Hounds in the Balkans" appeared in *Anthropology News*, volume 47, issue 5. I am grateful as well for the variety of funding I have received for my research in Bulgaria over the years from Bowdoin College, the National Science Foundation, the

American Council for Learned Societies, the International Research and Exchanges Board (IREX), Fulbright, the National Council for Eurasian and East European Research (NCEEER), the Woodrow Wilson International Center for Scholars, the Institute for Advanced Study in Princeton, and the Radcliffe Institute for Advanced Study at Harvard. I also want to thank those at Bowdoin who helped me to administer all of these grants: Ann Ostwald, Agnes McGrail, Cara Martin-Tetreault, and Kathi Lucas. At Duke University Press, special acknowledgment goes out to my editor, Courtney Berger, for being such a steadfast ally of this project and to the two anonymous readers whose comments so improved the final product. The efforts of Christine Choi, Jade Brooks, and Rebecca Fowler at Duke are also deeply appreciated, as is the skillful copyediting of Alex Wolfe.

I am blessed with many friends, mentors, and fabulous colleagues who enrich my life both intellectually and emotionally; they are too many to name and I want to thank them all for their encouragement and support over the years. In particular, Scott, Hayden, and Josephine have become my new and steadfast allies in the hunt for Venusian dust particles and the instigators of spontaneous strobe-light dance parties, for which I am eternally grateful. Most importantly, I want to thank my weird and wonderful daughter, the werepoodle. I think she is one of the silliest people on earth, and being her mom is the greatest pleasure I know.

In September of 1989 I dropped out of college and left the country because I thought the world was going to end. I was only nineteen years old and had little money. I was alone and knew no one in Europe, but none of that really mattered. There were enough nuclear weapons on the planet to destroy the Earth a thousand times over. In retrospect, it was a crazy decision, and it was one that would end up shaping the rest of my life. Of course, I had no idea of this at the time.

You see, I gained political consciousness during the Reagan era; I was the child of a Cold War going hot. Growing up in San Diego, I was surrounded by the children of soldiers in all four branches of the American military. The kids at my school were all vaguely aware that the next war might be the last one humans ever fought. I think I watched the 1983 television film *The Day After* at a particularly vulnerable age. The graphic representation of a nuclear attack on the United States scared the hell out of me. After the movie there was a special ABC *News Viewpoint* program discussing the pros and cons of nuclear weapons. The panel guests were Henry Kissinger, Carl Sagan, Brent Scowcroft, William F. Buckley Jr., Elie Wiesel, and Robert McNamara. During the debate, I remember Carl Sagan explaining that the nuclear arms race between the United States and the Soviet Union was like "two men standing waist deep in gasoline; one with three matches, the other with five." It was a vivid and effective mental image that seared into my young mind how close we already were to the brink of planetary annihilation.

I am not sure exactly when it happened, but at some point before I turned fourteen, I decided that it was unlikely that I would live to see twenty-five. Given the proliferation of missiles on either side of the Iron Curtain, I was pretty convinced that the entire world was going to be destroyed in a nuclear holocaust. This would make me a particularly nihilistic adolescent. Since the whole Earth was inevitably going to be reduced to a smoldering ash heap, there was really no point to anything. I was not alone in this feeling; a lot of my friends also rationalized not doing their homework because our city would certainly be hit in the first round of any nuclear attack.

I had a lot of questions about the political ideologies whose incommensurability had created this situation. So I joined the Model United Nations Club in middle school. This was a club filled mostly with geeky boys trying to intellectualize their way out of the discomforts of puberty. Model United Nations (MUN) was like a competitive debate team. We had conferences at other schools where discerning social studies teachers judged our role-playing abilities. Each school participating in a conference would be allocated a certain number of countries, and the school would have to provide a minimum of three representatives for each country—one for the General Assembly, one for an ad hoc political committee, and one for the Economic and Social Council. In addition, most school teams were given one country with a seat on the Security Council. If the school team was really lucky, it would be assigned a country that was one of the five permanent members of the Security Council: the United States, France, the United Kingdom, China, and the USSR. This was every middle school MUNer's dream: veto power.

For each assigned country, a team of three or four students would have to research the foreign policy of its government and its past voting record at the real United Nations in New York in order to role-play that country effectively at the student conference. In all of their spare time, the boys in my club would study up on the United States, Britain, and France, praying fervently that we would be asked to represent one of the veto wielding "good guys" at our next conference. No one wanted to be China, because all they ever did was abstain. And no one wanted to be the Union of

Soviet Socialists Republics, because they were the bad guys. No one, that is, save for me.

Maybe it was because I was a girl and I knew that they would never give me the chance to role-play a "good" country with veto power, or maybe it was because I was a contrarian, but I became the Eastern Bloc specialist of our club. I was hoping that some day we would be assigned the USSR and that I would get a shot at the Security Council and a chance to win the gavel (the highest prize of the competition). I read voraciously about the Russians, about Marxism-Leninism, about the Soviet space program, and about collectivized agriculture. I read everything that I could get my hands on, hoping to understand the Soviet worldview so that I could more accurately represent them and convincingly argue their position on the key world issues of the day: the Middle East, Northern Ireland, and nuclear proliferation among others.

I learned that the Soviets believed in a centrally controlled economy, where the government owned all of the factories and productive units in society and guaranteed citizens lifetime full employment in exchange for their political obedience to the Communist Party. Most communist countries began this process by expropriating the wealth of the bourgeois class, basically taking the rich people's money by force and making it the state's property on behalf of the workers. This process of expropriation was usually achieved through violent revolution, and the Soviets supported leftist insurgencies across the globe, hoping to destroy the capitalists so that humankind could move on to the next phase of history. What fascinated me most as I read about these communist movements was that they always claimed a moral high ground. The insurgents always claimed that they represented the interests of the poor and downtrodden masses against the rich and privileged elites. No matter what the USSR did, they justified their actions by appealing to equality, economic rights, and social justice, a package of powerful concepts to have in my MUN tool kit.

As I slowly became the expert on Soviet foreign policy, arguing the Communists' position in all of our practice sessions, I was now guaranteed the assignment of a socialist bloc country if there was one in our school's allotment. Since almost all of the Eastern European countries followed the lead of the USSR, I could use the same Soviet rhetoric to represent any communist country (with the notable exception of Yugoslavia). My first socialist country was the Ukrainian Soviet Socialist Republic, which I played in the General Assembly. I played Poland and Romania on a couple of ad hoc committees and then was finally assigned to be Bulgaria on the Security Council. Although I did not have veto power, I would be one of only fifteen delegates. Having experience on the council would increase my chances of getting put on it a second time. This was my chance to shine!

I spent weeks after school preparing for the conference. In 1985 Bulgaria was a relatively small country about the size of Delaware with a population of about nine million. It bordered Greece and Turkey to the south, Yugoslavia to the west, and Romania to the north. Its entire eastern border was on the Black Sea. A part of the Ottoman Empire for over five hundred years, the country regained its independence in 1878. Bulgaria was allied with the Germans during both World War I and World War II. In 1944 communist freedom fighters took over the government with Soviet support. For two years the country was technically a communist monarchy, but in 1946 they ousted the young king and established the People's Republic of Bulgaria. By 1985 the country had been under the control of one man for over a quarter of a century, and it was one of the USSR's most faithful allies. As a founding member of both the Council for Mutual Economic Assistance (the Communist trading bloc) and the Warsaw Pact (the Communist mutual defense treaty), Bulgaria was at the core of the Eastern Bloc and always voted together with the USSR. This was going to be easy.

Being on the Security Council was an exhilarating experience. Since everyone was officially referred to as "the delegate from [country name]," most of us did not know each other by our real names. We addressed each other as the names of our respective countries. I was simply called "Bulgaria." The boy who was representing the USSR was a grade above me. He had long, thick, pale lashes that framed dark blue eyes. He wore a dark gray suit and a deep red tie with gold flecks and had mastered a fake Russian accent that he deployed with utmost confidence. I spent both days of the conference sitting next to him, and he would often lean over and whisper advice into my ear. On the second day he asked me, "Hey Bulgaria, you want to have lunch? We should strategize the socialist position on Israel in order to avoid the US veto." We sat out on a bench together in the bright San Diego sun very seriously discussing Middle East politics while eating our peanut butter and jelly sandwiches. I felt no embarrassment at spending so much time with him and letting him give me directions. After all, I was Bulgaria. My role was to do what the USSR told me to do. After the conference, I told my girlfriends back at school that I had quite literally developed a *huge* crush on the Soviet Union.

In the eleventh grade, I finally got my chance at veto power. My high school was allotted the Soviet Union, and I was chosen to represent the USSR on the Security Council. I had spent most of my teenage years preparing for this one opportunity, and I studied like a fiend, memorizing the last three years worth of *US News and World Report*. I also spent everyday after school carefully listening to the new LP of the Irish rock band U2, using the lead singer's midsong monologues about apartheid in South Africa or dictatorships in Latin America as a study guide. I had been tipped off that the band was popular among the college students, and that they often culled MUN scenarios from U2's lyrics.

On November 16, 1986, all of the pretend delegates of the Security Council at the University of California, San Diego (UCSD) all-high-school MUN conference were awakened at 3:00 a.m. for an emergency session. The scenario the college students had cooked up for us was a Soviet incursion into West Berlin. They gave us no explanation, only saying that there had been reports of Soviet troops pouring through the Brandenburg gate. As we all convened in the UCSD seminar room at 3:30 a.m., eyes still heavy with disrupted slumber, my head was spinning as I frantically tried to come up with some possible explanation for my adopted country's sudden aggression. The boy playing the United States was immediately recognized by the chair and launched into an impassioned condemnation of the Soviet Union.

Of course I knew the Soviets would officially claim that they were supporting some kind of domestic revolution that was being squelched, but I had no specifics about local politics in West Berlin to make a convincing case to the rest of the Security Council delegates. There was no Internet back then, no Google. We did not even have laptop computers. I had to make something up. I had to think fast. The boy playing the United States was hungry for the gavel and this was my chance to steal it out from under his nose. I might never get a chance again.

The Security Council chair, a college student representing Ecuador who was also the judge, listened intently to the United States. The boy said nothing surprising or original, just a bunch of hackneyed lines about Soviet aggression, the situation in Afghanistan, and the global threats of totalitarianism and communism. The other high school students were still too sleepy to pay much attention at this point; the delegate from Senegal wiped some crusted mucus from the corner of his left bloodshot eye and sat rolling it around between his thumb and forefinger, clearly wishing he could be back in bed. To my right the boy representing Papua New Guinea was actually asleep, his chin pinned to his chest.

The United States finished his speech with a dramatic flailing of his arms, his eyes resting on mine, challenging me to respond. The chair also looked in my direction and asked, "Would the delegate from the Union of Soviet Socialist Republics care to make an opening statement?"

In a moment of panic and inspiration, I reached down under the table and removed one of my tennis shoes. I first slammed it on the table in front of me, and then hurled it across the room at the United States, shouting "You bourgeois, imperialist pig!"

Everyone in the room stared at me. Papua New Guinea's head shot up; Senegal flicked his eye crust across the table. Ecuador's mouth stood open. He looked to me, to the United States, and then to me. I thought I saw the corners of his thin mouth turn slightly upward. "Will the delegate from the Soviet Union kindly keep her footwear out of the debate?"

I smiled at him, confident that he had gotten the Khrushchev reference. I cleared my throat. "Capitalism and communism are thesis and antithesis. The conflict between them is inevitable, as is the progress of history. Only through conflict and confrontation can humankind reach its fullest potential, reach a new synthesis of political freedom and social justice," I said, the Hegelian dialectics plunging uncomfortably from my tongue into the college seminar room. But I had everyone's attention after the shoe. I continued, leaning both of my hands on the table in front of me and meeting the sleepy stares of the other fourteen delegates. My strategy was to convince them that a nuclear confrontation was inevitable given the buildup of intercontinental ballistic missiles (ICBMs) on both sides. Either there would be a nuclear war or there wouldn't. The Soviets were finally calling the bluff.

I knew the rules of this game well. The college students had prepared a scenario for us. As long as I stayed within the boundaries of political plausibility, I could introduce whatever justifications I wanted. I glanced at the gavel in the hand of the chair. I might just be able to win. It was a risky move on my part, but I really believed that a nuclear war between the superpowers was solidly within the realm of political plausibility. The question was: would the judges think so, too?

"The number of nuclear weapons currently in existence far exceeds the amount necessary to kill off the majority of the world's population and destroy all major cities across the globe," I said. "It now seems clear that the final conflict between capitalism and communism is inevitable. The Soviet leadership believes that the sooner this conflict occurs, the sooner communism can triumph over the bourgeois, imperialist phase of human history. The resolution of this conflict is both necessary and inevitable. History will show the United States to be the imperialist aggressor it is. A total nuclear assault on the part of both existing superpowers will destroy all private property, which will allow what is left of the human race to begin with a clean slate with no preexisting class divisions in society."

I stopped once more and took a deep breath. The chair was nodding his head at me. I stood up straight, pushing my chest out toward the United States. "In short, ladies and gentlemen of the Security Council, the leadership of the Soviet Union has only initiated the inevitable: the total destruction of both the United States and the Soviet Union, so that human history will more quickly process to its logical conclusion, the ultimate triumph of social justice in a true proletarian democracy! Our nuclear arsenal stands fully armed and ready to meet any US aggression."

The chair and the other kids in the room stared at me in awe. Senegal slapped his hand over his mouth. The delegate from the United States was immediately recognized and spat accusations of irrationality and aggression at me, and I could tell that he was a hawkish type. I felt that the other sixteen- and seventeen-year-olds in the room had bought into my scenario and taken my side. This outcome probably seemed inevitable to many of them, too. Whereas the MUN conference organizers had probably expected a garden-variety resolution condemning Soviet aggression, which would be vetoed by the USSR, I had single-handedly precipitated a mock nuclear holocaust by taunting the US delegate into launching a first strike. I then launched a retaliatory strike, firing ICBMS at all major metropolitan areas in North America and Western Europe. By the end of the session, the delegates of my Security Council unanimously passed a resolution condemning all nuclear weapons, even as we collectively realized that we had started the Third World War. The last paragraph of our resolution contained a warning to future generations not to repeat the mistakes we had made.

Out of four hundred or so high school kids, the judges decided that I was the most prepared and most persuasive delegate, even though I had destroyed the world. They, too, believed that nuclear war between the United States and the USSR was solidly within the realm of political possibility. They awarded me the gavel. When I went up to receive my much coveted prize, I was elated. It was one of the most important moments in my life thus far. I was almost certain, however, that I would never be able to share it with grandchildren of my own.

As the decade wore on, my fear of nuclear war continued to grow, seeming ever more inevitable. The only distraction was school and my newfound obsession with U2 and their politically engaged rock music. As the band's popularity grew in the late 1980s, I found a community of like-minded kids among my fellow U2 fans; they knew about world events and took the possibility of nuclear annihilation seriously. In the year after I won the gavel, I attended four U2 shows in Southern California and Arizona and learned about organizations like Greenpeace and Amnesty International from the tables at these concerts. I was impressed that there were people trying to change things but could never let go of the idea that it probably wouldn't make any difference in the end. Still, for a few hours, I could forget about Mutual Assured Destruction and let myself be a normal teenage girl.

Just under two years later, I started my first year of college in September 1988. After only nine months, I dropped out. What was the point of studying and getting good grades to earn a degree when the human race might soon be reduced to living in caves? Even though I had a full scholarship and enjoyed my classes at UC Santa Cruz, it seemed foolish to waste what little time I thought I had left learning about the world from books when I could be seeing it for real. I worked three different jobs in the summer of 1989 to save enough money to fund my travels. I bought a one-way ticket to Madrid and left at the end of September. I knew that someone was bound to launch those nukes eventually. How pathetic would it be if the world ended while I was sitting somewhere taking an exam? Backpacking around the globe sounded like the better thing to do.

I spent five weeks in the fall of 1989 traveling around Spain and Portugal, but the train tickets were more expensive than I thought and it would soon be too cold to camp out. I would need more money if I were to keep on traveling indefinitely. I had to find a job. An Australian traveler in Lisbon told me that I would be able to find good work as a nanny in London for the winter months. It would be expensive to get to London, and I would be close to broke if I did not find a job right away. It was a risk, but I did not know what else to do.

I went to Barcelona and found the bus station. I bought a one-way ticket to London, kissing it for luck. It was already early November, and I hoped that I could hole up in the UK for a few months until I saved up enough money to head down to Israel. It sounded like a good plan, but I was nervous. I was nineteen and alone in a bus station in Spain heading to London where I knew no one, hoping to find illegal work so I would not have to go home.

There was a small television mounted to the far corner of the bus station. I had not really paid any attention to it; they were showing some kind of cheesy Spanish soap operas. I was recording in my journal all of the details of the people I had met and the places I had been over the past few weeks when I noticed some of the other waiting passengers standing up to get closer to the TV. At first it was just a few people, but slowly a crowd started to form. There was whispering at first, then a loud murmur, and finally an excited chatter that made me wonder what was so interesting. I looked up, but the TV was too far away and I was too nearsighted to get a sense of what was going on. It was only when the two women behind the ticket counter and the people standing in line to buy tickets all wandered over to the little TV that I stood up to join the crowd.

There were people jumping up and down on the Berlin Wall.

For a moment I was sure that this was some kind of movie until I noticed that the little words in the upper corner of the screen said "Live from Berlin" in Spanish. The voice of the Spanish newscaster was incredulous as he described the scene. East Germans were flooding into West Berlin and no one was stopping them. Could it really be?

If I had had the money, I would have gotten on the next bus to Berlin. I promised myself then that I would go as soon as I had enough of a cushion to buy a plane ticket home if I needed one. I did find a job in England for three months and after that spent a month working on a kibbutz in Israel. I passed that whole winter following the news as one former communist country after another embraced democracy without interference from the Russians.

In early June of 1990 I found myself in Turkey after having traveled overland from Egypt through Jordan, Iraq, and Syria. I was a seasoned traveler now with a money belt full of British pounds and a knack for finding the cheapest hotels and surviving on bread, tomatoes, cheese, and water. The time had finally come. I applied at the Bulgarian consulate in Istanbul for a visa to visit my first communist country. The Bulgarians would have none of me; they only offered a thirty-hour transit visa so that I could take the train to either Yugoslavia or Romania. I flipped a coin and chose Yugoslavia.

As I boarded the train in Istanbul, I did not know what to expect. I had spent so many years studying the communist world for MUN, but I could not conjure up in my mind what that world might actually look like. The only thing I could imagine was some kind of Orwellian dystopia with no colors and people all dressed in exactly the same clothes. Would it look like one big jail? Or perhaps one big work camp? Over two decades later, I still remember that train ride as if it were yesterday. Once out of Turkey I was surprised to see the lush green Bulgarian countryside, punctuated with vibrant yellow fields of sunflowers. The cities were great sprawling expanses of grayness, but they were sprinkled with the varied colors of laundry hung out to dry on the balconies of the identical apartment blocks.

My longest stop in Bulgaria was in Plovdiv, the country's second largest city. On the way into the station, I had caught sight of one balcony in particular and spent some time in my compartment wondering about the people who lived there. It was a breezy day and there was laundry flapping restlessly in the wind. I had seen that there were two T-shirts (one red, one greenish), some dark socks, and what looked like it might be a pair of jeans or a pair of dark blue trousers. As I stared out the window I thought about the people that these clothes belonged to. I thought about the woman who had probably hung this laundry out to dry. These were ordinary people. Maybe there was a man and a woman and a couple of kids who had to do laundry like everyone else. They wore socks, which got smelly and needed to be washed.

It was such a mundane fact but it struck me like a lightning bolt. After all of those years of thinking about the Soviet Union and trying to understand how Communist leaders would respond to certain international crises in Security Council deliberations, it had never occurred to me to think about their socks. Those big Communists went home, took off their socks, and threw them in some pile of dirty clothes. They probably lost socks like I did. It was perfectly possible that some members of the Politburo went to work wearing an odd match. How could I have missed this basic fact that made

The author in Berlin in July 1990.

all of these people so much like me? In the midst of totalitarian oppression, people still had to wash their socks. For all of my research and fascination with the Communist bloc, I never stopped to think about the fact that there was a whole world of normality that had been hidden behind the rhetoric of the Cold War.

In that first summer after what most East Europeans simply called the Changes, I traveled through Yugoslavia, Romania, Hungary, Czechoslovakia, and the German Democratic Republic for the better part of two months. It was a land of euphoria as young people took to the streets to test the limits of their newfound freedoms. For a twenty-year-old American with a newfound fascination for socks, I threw myself into the tumult of youthful jubilation that accompanied that summer. There were other Western travelers like me, curious to see what life was like behind the now crumbling Iron Curtain, but I spent my time with the young East Europeans, talking about music and food and sex and cigarette brands and movies and the places we wanted to travel to. We told jokes and laughed politely even when they were untranslatable. We marveled at how much our respective governments had tried to convince us that we should be enemies and how easy it was for us to become friends.

I was there, celebrating the end of an era, ecstatically toasting a future that I believed would be filled with peace and prosperity for all. The ugliness and brutality of the East European totalitarian regimes was finally gone. Where there had been dictatorship, there would now be democratic elections. Where there had been one state-controlled media, there would now be freedom of the press. Where there had been secret police and persecution, there would now be freedom of speech and assembly. Where there had been exit visas, there would now be freedom of travel. Where there had been shortages of basic goods, there would now be an endless consumer bonanza. With the hot July sun on our backs and a hearty dose of newfound ambition in our hearts, my new friends and I traded visions of a better world, exchanged addresses, and promised to keep in touch.

The world was not going to end.

Lucky for me, I was able to get back into college and to continue with my studies. Without the imminent fear of nuclear war my life became lighter, and for the first time I allowed myself to think about what I might like to do with my future. I wondered if my new friends in Eastern Europe were doing the same thing. Nine years would pass before I would return to the former Eastern Bloc for the second time—this time to the country that would not let me stay the first time. I was a graduate student at UC Berkeley and was trying to decide on a place to do fieldwork for my dissertation research. I had also met a young Bulgarian law student. It was a mixture of intellectual curiosity and infatuation that would lead me back to Bulgaria in January and March of 1998.

During those first two visits I was shocked to realize that the hopes and dreams of 1990 had not been realized. Although most people were still glad that communism was gone and agreed that the totalitarian past was best put behind them, the promises of democracy had not been realized. Many Bulgarians I met had started to question the transition process. Where there had been guaranteed full employment, there were now hundreds of thousands of people without work. Where there had been security and order, there was now chaos and unchecked criminal violence. Where there had been universal health care, the best doctors now worked in fee-only clinics for the new rich. Where there had been free university education, there were now private colleges. Where there had been a decent amount of gender equality, there was now outright discrimination against women. Where there had once been stable families and communities, there was now an exodus of the young and qualified who sought better fortunes in the West. One taxi driver explained to me that "when you build a new house, you usually live in your old one while the new one is under construction." In Bulgaria, he said, they had torn down the old house (communism) before the new one (capitalism) was ready. Everyone was now forced to live on the street.

Those of us living in the West heard very little about this during the 1990s. The news focused on high-level perspectives about the success of democracy and the triumphs of free markets in the region. Once more the lives (and socks) of ordinary people were left out of the story. It was clear to me in 1998 that there were people suffering in Bulgaria, that *democratzia* was not all that it was cracked up to be. From that wondrous summer in 1990 emerged a dark reality. People who had worked hard and built success-ful careers under the old system were cheated out of their well-deserved retirement. Men and women in the middle of their lives had to drastically change course just to stay afloat; they had to learn new skills, new lan-guages, and an entirely new way of thinking. A whole generation of young people lost the futures for which they had been preparing themselves. Entire academic disciplines disappeared overnight; what do you do with a PhD in Marxist economics or dialectical materialism in a capitalist society? In short, daily life had been turned on its head. No one knew what the rules were anymore. And those most willing to test the boundaries were the ones who found themselves on top.

In the decades since 1989 much scholarly ink has been spilt on the Changes, what Western academics preferred to call "the economic tran-sition" or the "economic transformation." A whole new discipline of so-called transitology was created to allow economists, political scientists, anthropologists, sociologists, modern historians, and interested policymak-ers to study the processes through which the former centrally planned economies became free market ones and through which dictatorships be-came democracies. Hundreds of dissertations were written on how to create stock exchanges and liberalize markets; when to reform the judiciary and what to do with Communist archives; whom to ban from public service and why it was necessary to restitute property previously expropriated by the Communists. Scholars puzzled over how to create civil society, promote political pluralism, fight corruption, protect minorities, and prevent civil war or ethnic conflict, particularly after the debacle that was the breakup of the former Yugoslavia. Certainly these were very important questions. Understanding as momentous a social change as the transformation of communist societies into capitalist ones required a grand perspective.

But there was something that the nationally representative survey samples were missing and something that seemed more important to me than any of these other questions. Something that was more personal. I wanted to know: What was happening to the ordinary people who had to live through these changes? What had happened to the two Czech girls that I had camped with outside of Prague, or to the Serbian philosophy students with whom I debated Locke and Hume over a bottle of cheap red wine in that park in the center of Belgrade? Did they finish university, too? Were they married? Did they have children? Did they have jobs? Were they even still alive? Were things better now? Were they worse?

Thankfully, I was one of a whole new cohort of anthropologists and qualitative sociologists, both Western and East European, who set out to explore what had happened to the little people who had been "lost" in the transition. Over the twenty years that I have been visiting the region, my favorite souvenirs have always been the personal stories that I collected along the way. At first, they were scribbled out on the backs of dinner napkins or surreptitiously scratched out onto little note pads. Later, after I received more formal ethnographic training in graduate school, I became a compulsive writer of field notes, sitting down at my computer every night for an hour before allowing myself to go to sleep. I sometimes asked questions, but mostly I just listened. In bars and restaurants, in parks and plazas, in hotel lobbies and private kitchens, people seemed more than willing to talk about their daily lives. In English or in Bulgarian or in some crazy combination of sign language and polyglotinous grunting, I tried to understand what people were feeling about the unprecedented changes that were happening all around them. It was a curiosity that would become a career.

I also watched my own ideas and opinions start to shift as I was sucked in and shaped by the social and economic upheavals around me. How could I have possibly remained immune? I was no mere scholar in Bulgaria. I married that Bulgarian law student from Berkeley and was slowly immersed into a massive constellation of familial relationships that took me years to figure out. I became the progenitor of a new half-American, half-Bulgarian citizen, sharing all of the anxieties of motherhood with women

Роден(а) на 26.04.1970

Държава САЩ

Гражданство САЩ

Влязъл в страната на 27.09.99

УДОСТОВЕРЕНИЕТО Е ИЗДАДЕНО

от СДВР .... у-ние на МВР

гр СОФИЯ ....

на 22.10.99 Важи до 21.10.2000

за ПРО ДЪЛЖИТЕЛНО .... пребиваване
(временно, постоянно)

в гр. (с) СОФИЯ

печат СДВР (подпис)

№ 0204736

ИМЕ ФИЛИПОВ
(на кирилица – по реда на записване

КРИСТЕН
в задграничния паспорт на чужденеца)

ГОДСИ
(на латиница – както са записани

в задграничния паспорт на чужденеца)

ЕНЧ

The author's Bulgarian personal identity card from 1999. Note that it is forbidden to smile in photos used for official Bulgarian documents.

from all walks of life. As a parent, I constantly worried about what the years ahead would hold for my daughter and wondered what I could do to try to prepare her for what seemed to be an unpredictable future. Many of the women I met were also scared and unsure of the rules in this new capitalist world. They had no idea what values or talents to encourage in their children to help them survive. The rules were constantly shifting. I wanted to make sense of things for them as much as I wanted to make sense of things for myself.

Writing down the details of people's varied experiences, the things they said and did and how other people reacted to their actions, helped me to keep track of all of the cultural information I was taking in every day. Years later when I found myself in front of a college classroom, I learned that sharing anecdotes from these notes helped to make me a more effective teacher. Rather than trying to explain the shortcomings of command economics from a theoretical point of view, I often told my students stories of what it had been like to go shopping for cosmetics or clothing in Bulgaria before and after the Changes. Instead of trying to catalogue all of the different policies that communist governments had put into place to promote equality between men and women, I would share with them the life

Two Bulgarian girls in traditional dress in the Rhodope Mountain town of Smolyan.

histories of real Bulgarian women who managed to have both families and careers under the old system and the many challenges they later faced with the advent of free markets.

I soon learned that young people could study communism in their modern history textbooks, but they were not really able to grasp that it had been a "normal," functioning system without seeing it through the eyes of the individuals who had lived within it. In my classes I wanted to teach my students about these different ways of viewing the world. Although the actual practice of communism in Eastern Europe had failed miserably, there were generations of men and women who had been raised to think about the world in a very different way, shaping their choices and forging their lives within a system that operated by a set of rules that they all knew and understood. And then one day it was gone. My students seemed fundamentally unable to comprehend the sheer magnitude of that change. I

An ad for a Bulgarian beer that simply says "Men know why." When asked, most Bulgarians don't actually know why.

asked them: How do people continue with life after the total destruction of the political and economic system within which they spent their entire lives? What happened to the state-owned enterprises where they worked? What happened to the money they had saved or to the pensions they had earned? What happened to their cities, their schools, their playgrounds, to the cemeteries where some of the tombstones bore red stars instead of crosses?

The scope of the Changes was immense. In the course of a few short years, hard-earned college degrees in Eastern Europe were rendered useless, massive enterprises went bankrupt, life savings were eaten up by hyperinflation and banking collapses while the promise of a comfortable retirement evaporated. The anthropologist Alexei Yurchak wrote a book about the last Soviet generation called *Everything Was Forever Until It Was No More*. This brilliant title captures the fascination that must inevitably accompany any study of the events of 1989. Why didn't anyone see it coming?

I am always amazed by the stories of the men and women who decided to become official members of the Bulgarian Communist Party on November 8, 1989. I am shocked by the tales of the people who risked their lives to defect to the West just weeks before the wall came down. And what about the desperate souls who committed suicide just days before the entire world changed around them? Having lost all hope that he would ever find freedom or happiness, some young man killed himself perhaps just hours before communism collapsed. Yurchak's title reminds us that there are many circumstances in our lives that can seem rigid and unchangeable but that are actually contingent and unstable. Things around us can seem like they will be there forever; we only realize their ephemerality once they are gone.

Of course, with the flow of information controlled by authoritarian governments, it is understandable that East Europeans did not know everything that was going on in their countries. In the Soviet Union the Communists had been in power for more than seventy years. In Eastern Europe they had been in control for the better part of four decades. Bulgaria had the same head of state, Todor Zhivkov, for about thirty-five years. Given the stranglehold these governments had on the political system, it makes sense that people might believe that everything was forever.

But this blindness to the possibility of the Soviet imperial collapse was ubiquitous in the West as well. In the United States alone billions of dollars had been spent collecting intelligence on the Soviet Union and training generations of Sovietologists to help the American government understand what was happening on the ground behind the Iron Curtain. But politicians and scholars in the West were just as surprised as Eastern European citizens. Indeed, the entire world was more or less caught off guard by the relatively unspectacular resolution of the Cold War, a war that many of us believed would end in the total destruction of the Earth. We got barely a whimper when we were expecting a bang. How had I ever become so convinced that the Cold War would end with total nuclear annihilation? How could I have been so blinded to the possibility that everything might eventually work itself out? These are questions that have been bugging me for the last twenty years.

Looking back on the transition from communism helps us to remember that the future is always contingent, and the rules of the game today may be very, very different tomorrow. Teaching about the collapse of communism is one way to get young people to understand that the way the world is now is not the way it has always been, nor the way it will always be. More importantly, seeing the world as it *is* should not prevent us from imagining

A socialist-era statue in Sofia.

how the world could (or perhaps should) be. The Slovenian philosopher Slavoj Žižek really put his finger on something when he said that it is far easier for young people today to imagine total planetary environmental catastrophe than it is for them to imagine any significant changes in the political and economic system that will precipitate this catastrophe. How would we fare if capitalism suddenly disappeared? Few people even think to ask themselves this question. Yet there are millions of men and women still alive today who experienced the practical equivalent.

History teaches us that empires rise and fall, but the scale of the communist collapse was unprecedented. Within a few short years the maps of Eastern Europe and Central Asia had to be completely redrawn to accommodate the new countries that appeared following the implosion of the Soviet Union and the Yugoslav wars. People who once lived together in a country called the USSR would be spread across fifteen new nations. People who once called themselves Yugoslavians would now be Serbians, Croatians, Bosnians, Slovenes, Macedonians, Montenegrins, and most recently Kosovars. Czechoslovakians became Czechs and Slovaks. East Germans were reduced to just being *ossies* (Easterners) in a newly unified Germany, their country swallowed up by the West. Even countries like Romania, Poland, Hungary, or Bulgaria, which remained geographically intact at the national level, did not escape the frenzy of renaming that swept across the former communist world. The names of streets, squares, universities, towns, and cities were commonly changed to reflect the coming of the new democratic era. An ordinary person could easily begin to feel like a stranger in the place were she had spent her entire life.

Of course, there were different circumstances in each of the Eastern Bloc countries, and they all faced specific challenges as they emerged into new democratic states. Although there were many differences, there were also many similarities, particularly in the ways in which ordinary people experienced changes on the ground. The focus in this book is mostly on Bulgaria because it is the country where I have spent the most time. Admittedly, Bulgaria was one of the closest allies of the USSR, and it is one of the countries that has fared least well since 1989—this does in some ways make the experience of Bulgarians unique. But Bulgaria also shared the same political and economic system with its socialist brother countries, and this system was dismantled at the same historical moment in the same geopolitical circumstances, upending an entire way of life to which people had become accustomed. The disappearance of the welfare state, the re-vocation of the promise of lifetime employment, the privatization of public property, the creation of free markets, the rise of new nationalisms, and the growing nostalgia for the past are characteristic of all countries emerging from communism. Thus, thinking about the Changes in Bulgaria can pro-vide a lens through which to examine the process of economic and political transition more broadly.

Perhaps more importantly, Bulgaria is a country about which most Westerners have few preconceived notions. Unlike Russia or Poland or the former Yugoslavia, Bulgaria has seldom been in the international spotlight, and few people know much about this relatively small country tucked into the most southeastern corner of Europe. Even with all of my background in current events, I did not know what to expect of Bulgaria when I first boarded that train in Istanbul back in June of 1990. It was the beginning of a journey to Belgrade, but I had no idea back then that it was also the beginning of a journey that would consume the next two decades of my life.

CHAPTER 1 **CONTRABAND, 1990**

I had already been in the compartment with the five Yugoslavs for almost two hours when I noticed the unlabeled cardboard boxes tucked behind their legs underneath their seats. The Bulgarian border police had just entered the train. I watched the young men all sit up straight, pressing their knees together in a vain attempt to hide the boxes from view. As the surly uniformed officer collected our passports, I realized that I was in a lot of trouble. I was sharing a train compartment with smugglers. They might be smuggling drugs. The Bulgarians would surely think that I was one of them, and I would end up in a dark communist jail cell until some underpaid American diplomat found the time to rescue me.

When I realized that I was in a compartment with smugglers, my first thought was to grab my rucksack and get out as soon as possible. But by the time I managed to get my things in order, the Bulgarian border police were already walking past our compartment down to the first compartment on our train. One of the officers glanced in and made eye contact with me. He had already seen where I was sitting. It would look suspicious to move now.

Maybe it was nothing, I told myself. This was my first time in a communist country, and I didn't know how things worked. Maybe they were smuggling banned books or bootlegged Western cassette tapes. Maybe it was some special kind of booze. Perhaps it would just be confiscated. As much as I tried to tell myself that I was overreacting, my mind kept imagining the worst, that those sealed unmarked boxes were full of drugs. If the Yugoslavs were caught, it would be difficult for me to explain that I had nothing to do with them before finding the free seat in their compartment back in Istanbul.

I shuddered at the thought that I might end up in some cold, gray Bulgarian prison. Unlike the other former communist countries in June of 1990, Bulgaria was still quite unwelcoming to foreigners, especially Americans. Since I was traveling from Istanbul to Belgrade on a thirty-hour transit visa, I could not register with the American Embassy in Sofia. No one knew that I was here. In fact, nobody at home had any idea where I was. I told my mother that I was leaving Turkey, but I had not given her the details of my trip through Bulgaria by train. I had written a few letters to friends telling them that I was planning to go to Eastern Europe, but I told others that I would be going from Turkey directly to Greece.

But here I was in Bulgaria with five young men that I did not know. Perhaps they were hoping that my presence would distract the border and customs police. Or perhaps they might just say that the boxes were all mine if they got caught, that I had hired them to help me smuggle whatever it was I was supposed to be smuggling. I kept thinking of all of the horror stories of tourists who have drugs slipped into their luggage and get arrested. I was only twenty. I did not want to go to prison.

These young men did not look like smugglers back when I boarded the train. It was early June, and I had been traveling alone through Europe and the Middle East for the last nine months. I had a system for choosing what kind of people were the safest to share a compartment with, a system that maximized personal security and minimized the potential risk of harassment. For any given train journey I was planning to make, I would get to the platform early and watch as other people boarded the train, carefully scanning the crowd for families and old women, the safest compartment mates. I would always board the train just five minutes before departure, even if it meant the possibility of not getting a seat. As a young woman traveling alone, the biggest mistake you could make would be to sit in a compartment before the train was fully boarded. In that case, you had no control over whom you shared the compartment with.

The problem on this particular journey from Istanbul to Belgrade was that almost all of the passengers on the train were men. There were no

The author's thirty-hour transit visa from 1990.

families. There were hardly any women at all. Traveling from the Middle East and NATO-controlled Turkey through Warsaw Pact member state Bulgaria to nonaligned Yugoslavia by train was apparently not yet a common occurrence for ordinary Turks. Furthermore, while other countries had immediately opened up after the fall of the Berlin Wall in November 1989, Bulgaria stayed stubbornly closed, waiting to see what would happen in the Soviet Union (which would not finally collapse until 1991). I had just over a day to get through my first communist country. I had to choose my compartment wisely.

I waited until about five minutes before the train was going to depart, watching the steady stream of men board the train from the platform. I was wearing very loose cotton khaki pants and an untucked man's shirt. My hair was tied back in a bun at the nape of my neck. I wore no cosmetics or jewelry. My feet were shod in worn Birkenstock sandals. These were my traveling clothes, as androgynous as possible. I was also quite emaciated at that time, having suffered from a terrible bout of dysentery in Syria.

I boarded the train and walked down the narrow corridor peering through the glass into the various compartments. There was no one yet crowding the aisles; the train would not be full. I could take my time deciding where I wanted to sit. Most of the compartments were occupied by an assortment of middle-aged men who, in my experience, would be the most lecherous toward a woman traveling alone. At my tender age of twenty, I had come up with what I called the Universal Law of Men, which helped me choose train compartments. As men in all cultures gained weight and replaced the hair on their heads with thick carpets of hair on their backs, they were more likely to come untied at the sight of a young woman traveling alone, assuming her to be a prostitute or libertine of some kind. Old men might stare at me, but in those pre-Viagra days they were almost entirely harmless. Young men might try to flirt with me, and there was always the danger that they would take rejection badly, but for the most part they were the least likely to be interested in a woman dressed as boyishly as I was. The key thing with young men was to deal with them only in groups of three or more. Groups of young men inevitably included a leader, a top dog, and as long as the leader was a good guy, the others would be fine, too.

And so it was that I chose a compartment with five young men who looked to me like students. I guessed that they were between the ages of twenty and twenty-three. The first one was a handsome blond man with an angular face and light peach fuzz on his chin and upper lip. He wore jeans, an AC/DC T-shirt, and what looked like a knockoff pair of Converse high-top sneakers. Across from him was another blond man. I later learned that his name was Goran. The other three young men in the compartment were slightly darker than the first two, with deep brown eyes and longish brown hair. They also wore jeans, and one wore a frayed Beatles T-shirt. They all looked to the man in the AC/DC shirt when I pulled open the compartment door and pointed to the free seat nearest to the corridor.

The AC/DC guy (whose name was Sasha) said something to Goran in Serbo-Croatian. Goran then looked to me.

"Speak English?"

"Yes."

"Where from?"

"USA," I answered. "I am going to Belgrade."

Their eyes all seemed to widen simultaneously. They looked from Sasha to me, back to Sasha, and back to me.

"USA?" said Goran, "Jimi Hendrix? The Doors?"

"Yes, USA. Bruce Springsteen." I smiled. "May I sit with you?"

Sasha nodded to Goran while eyeing me with his pale blue eyes. He was very fair and Slavic looking; he looked like what I imagined a Russian would look like.

"Please sit down," Goran said, gesturing to the free seat. "We have long journey."

I hoisted my rucksack up over my head to throw it onto the luggage rack. One of the darker boys stood up to help me.

"Thanks," I mumbled, as he wiggled my pack in between their duffle bags.

He replied with something in Serbo-Croatian that I assumed meant "you're welcome."

I sat down in the free seat, feeling for the money belt under my pants at my waist. Once the train started moving I would excuse myself and go to the bathroom. There I would remove my passport and train ticket before returning to the compartment. I had brought some bread and two bottles of water in my pack and hoped that I would be able to find some cheese along the way. If the young men had brought food with them, I did not see it. Instead, they were all clutching newly opened cartons of Marlboro Red cigarettes.

"My name is Kristen," I said, pointing to my chest.

"My name is Goran," said Goran. "He is Sasha."

The other young men introduced themselves as Pavle, Nikola, and Miloje. The train lurched forward. We sat in silence. Sasha then carefully opened a box of his new cigarettes, pulling several cigarettes so that they protruded out from the box. He offered them to me and said, "Smoke?"

"No, thank you," I said.

He proceeded to offer the box to all of the other men. One by one they each took a cigarette and fumbled for lighters in their jeans. In an instant, the compartment was filled with the smoke of five Marlboros.

"You go Belgrade?" Goran said.

"Yes. It is my first time in Yugoslavia."

"You meet someone?"

"Yes," I lied. "I am meeting my boyfriend."

"American?"

"Yes," I said. "He is American, too."

Goran nodded. Sasha said something in Serbo-Croatian.

Goran translated. "You like rock music?"

"Yes, of course. I love rock and roll. I am a huge U2 fan, you know, the Irish band."

At this, all five young men leaned forward, smiling at me.

"Yes, the Edge is a great guitarist," Goran said. "Do you like Yugoslav music?"

"I am sorry. I don't know any Yugoslav music."

Goran translated and the men nodded again, curls of gray smoke twirling toward the ceiling as they paused between their exhalations. The man directly across from me, called Pavle, was blowing smoke rings. Miloje, the man seated next to him between Pavle and Sasha (who was gazing out the window), was alternately blowing smoke out of the left and right corners of his mouth. Sasha did not need to do any smoking tricks to be cool. He was James Bond cool. It was clear from the way Goran deferred to him for everything that all of the men looked up to him. I imagined for a moment that he might be some kind of local rock star, but his white blond hair was too closely cropped for 1990. He looked as if he was in the military, or perhaps he had been recently discharged. He had perfect posture and a perfect body to match it. While the other young men reclined in several different variations on the standard male slouch, Sasha leaned back into his seat with his broad shoulders thrown back in a pose of confident defiance. He might have seemed very uptight with his rigid back and his short hair if it were not for his fashionably torn black jeans and the rows of leather bands wrapped around both of his wrists.

Across from him sat Nikola, the shaggiest looking of the lot. He had long, stringy hair that looked like it had not been washed in several days. Whereas Sasha's Slavic features were fine and angular, Nikola's eyes, nose, and cheeks almost seemed a caricature of the Slavic stereotype. His dark eyes were angled upward toward his temples making a perfectly parallel line with the steep diagonal of his cheekbones. His lips were thin, and his nose was narrow but tall. It seemed small from the front; his nostrils were close together under an almost delicate pointy tip. But in profile, his nose descended in a forty-five-degree angle from his brow, straight but somehow oddly out of proportion to the rest of his face. When smoking, Nikola inhaled the deepest. He was not smoking to look cool; he was smoking because his body craved the nicotine. When he spoke to Sasha in Serbo-Croatian, I could see that his teeth were the most yellow.

"Are you a student?" Goran asked me, trying to break the silence.

"Yes."

"Are you rich?" Goran asked.

I laughed. "No. Not really. I am just backpacking around," I said, pointing up at my rucksack.

"What do you study?"

"I don't know yet. Maybe political science."

"I study English," Goran explained. "Sasha is a physicist. He is very intelligent."

Upon hearing his name, Sasha looked up at me and nodded. It occurred to me that he probably understood English. He said something to Goran.

"He wants to know why you are alone." Goran translated.

"Well . . ."

"Are you a spy?" Goran interrupted.

At this I laughed again, feeling uncomfortable. "I am only twenty!" I said.

Sasha laughed, too. The other men in the compartment laughed with him, probably wondering what we were laughing at. Sasha crushed his cigarette out into the ashtray by the window. Outside, the Turkish countryside between Istanbul and the Bulgarian border was rushing past in a kind of impressionistic blur. It was a sunny day; the blue of the sky rested lightly on the greens and yellows of the fields. I wondered how long it would take us to get to Bulgaria and whether I should excuse myself to the bathroom to retrieve my ticket and passport.

Sasha spoke again.

"Why do you dress like a boy?" Goran asked.

It was a fair question. Sasha was now staring at me, looking at my plain face and my man's shirt.

"So that boys don't pay attention to me," I said directly to Sasha. Goran translated, but I think Sasha understood on his own. He smiled at me, nodding in understanding, and, at least in my mind, deciding that he would look out for me until we got to Belgrade. This made me feel comfortable (and added what I thought was more empirical evidence for my Universal Law of Men). I took a deep breath and let out a long sigh.

Goran opened a pack of his cigarettes, offering them to Sasha who immediately took one. He then offered one to Pavle, Miloje, and Nikola, and they all took one each. Goran turned to me, "Please join us. These are real Marlboro."

"No, thank you," I said. "I don't really smoke."

"But America is Marlboro country, no?"

I smiled. "Yes. I suppose it is."

"There are many cowboys, yes?"

I laughed at his question, shaking my head. A flash of confusion crossed his face as if he felt he had asked me something stupid. He looked to Sasha, who was also watching me with interest.

"Well," I said, "We still do have professional cowboys. Not as many as there used to be, but we still have some. Especially in places like Montana or Wyoming."

Goran took a long drag on his cigarette as if he were inhaling Montana and Wyoming through the thin barrel of packed tobacco. The end of the cigarette flared orange, and he breathed in. "I would like someday to go to America."

The conversation turned to the names of the places Goran wanted to visit. At the mention of the words *New York*, *Boston*, and *San Francisco* the other young men listened to us more intently, leaning forward in their seats. Goran explained that the five men were all grade school friends from Belgrade. He referred to himself as a Yugoslavian, and I was too young and naïve to ask what kind, although I later decided that they were probably Serbs. This was June 1990, still about a year before the Slovenes declared their independence, followed shortly thereafter by the Croatians. The secession of Croatia from Yugoslavia would lead to war, and that war would be greatly exacerbated by the subsequent secession of Bosnia-Herzegovina. But none of that had happened yet. Miloje wore a large crucifix around his neck, but I assumed that this was a fashion statement more than a religious symbol. They were in a band. Goran played the lead guitar, and Nikola was their bassist. Miloje was drummer, and Pavle played the keyboard. Sasha was the lead vocalist, writing all of the lyrics to their songs.

"Were you in Istanbul for a gig?" I asked, looking up to the luggage racks for signs of instruments.

"No, no," Goran said quickly, "Just visiting." He said this in such a defensive way that I understood I was not to press the question further. I looked at the five of them, and found myself wondering about their lives. Although I knew that Yugoslavia voted with the nonaligned countries in the General Assembly, I knew little about actual life in Yugoslavia. I also knew that before 1989 Yugoslavs could travel more freely than other communist citizens, but they still suffered from the kind of consumer shortages that were supposedly characteristic of the entire Eastern Bloc. The difference, of course, was that Yugoslavs could travel to Austria or Italy or Turkey to go shopping.

In most other East European nations, citizens needed an exit visa approved by the government in order to leave the country, and these visas were only issued if some family member was essentially held hostage back at home to guarantee the traveler's return. Many people had been trapped in their countries, unable to travel abroad or to emigrate at will. The Communists feared that the most educated and able (that is, the most able to survive and thrive in the capitalist West) would leave, depriving the society of valuable human capital and abandoning the less intelligent and less capable comrades to build socialism on their own.

As much as the communists wanted to believe that everyone was equal in value, there was no denying that ability and intelligence were variable even if you did everything to guarantee an equally high standard of education for everyone. Communist governments had gone a long way in leveling the playing field, but equal access to quality schools, adequate nutrition, and universal health care could not mitigate the reality that some people were just smarter, better looking, or more charismatic than others. These exceptional people would always believe that they deserved more. Their parents would also want them to have more, and this desire to have one's children succeed would often promote a system that encouraged nepotism despite the egalitarian dream.

Communists believed that all citizens had a duty to build the bright socialist future together and that those who had been endowed with exceptional personal gifts should use them for the good of the whole society, rather than merely for themselves. It was this doctrine of egalitarian fundamentalism that many Bulgarians, Romanians, Czechoslovaks, Russians, East Germans, Hungarians, and Poles wanted to escape; many would risk their life to do so, hoping to find a better future in the West. They imagined that the West was a place where their unique talents would be valued, appreciated, and rewarded, where meritocracy would replace gerontocracy, where skill and ability would replace seniority and loyalty to the Communist Party.

Yugoslav socialism had always been different from Soviet communism. One big thing that made Yugoslavia different was this relative lack of travel restrictions before 1989. People could leave if they wanted, but many of them chose not to. In my compartment were five young men, all healthy and educated, one apparently a highly intelligent physicist. In the course of our conversations, Goran told me that they had all visited Turkey several times before 1989. Turkey was a capitalist and NATO allied country, yet they had always gone back home. When Goran spoke of his hometown, Belgrade, he spoke of it in a way that made it clear that he intended to spend the rest of his life there. This was strange to me because everything I ever heard about the communist world was that people were desperate to get out.

I watched them curiously as they performed their smoking ritual. After each round of cigarettes was crushed out, one of them would open a pack and offer it around to the other four. One by one they would each take a cigarette. Miloje and Pavle would light them up right away. Goran would twirl his around in his fingers, admiring the brown and white paper and pinching at the filter. Nikola would tap his cigarette on the back of his hand, packing the tobacco toward the filter. He would play with his lighter, flicking at the wheel a few times before cupping his hand around the end of his Marlboro and lighting up as if to protect the flame from some imaginary breeze. Sasha would take the cigarette and store it behind his ear, nodding his head in thanks and then returning to his acute study of the passing countryside. Eventually, he would take out a box of matches and strike one, lighting the end of his cigarette, closing his eyes, and then savoring the first puff like it was a drug. This pattern continued over and over. It was only on the ninth round of cigarette offerings that it occurred to me that they might be nervous about something. It was an awful lot of chain smoking, even if the Marlboros were a special treat.

"Excuse me for a moment," I said, standing up to find the bathroom. I slid open the door and a cloud of smoke billowed out into the corridor. I walked down the hall and found the small lavatory, which was vacant. Once the door was locked behind me, I undid my leather belt and pulled out the hidden waist pouch that I always wore over the lower part of my stomach. Here I kept my passport, my American Express Traveler's Cheques, and three one hundred dollar bills for emergencies. My passport and the money were all curved to match the curve of my lower belly after having lived there for so long. Just as I was removing my passport and train ticket, I felt the train start to slow down. We were nearing the Bulgarian-Turkish border.

Within minutes the train stopped. I slid back into my compartment with the five Yugoslavs who were still smoking, although they seemed more agitated. The Bulgarian border police got on the train to start inspecting passports. Nikola and Goran kept glancing at Sasha who maintained a steady gaze out of the window. Miloje shuffled his feet. It was then that I noticed the boxes. There were three unmarked boxes under the seat and behind the legs of the men across from me. I glanced down beneath my own seat, and saw three more boxes under the bench on my side. The boxes were plain cardboard and were sealed with wide packing tape. Sasha said something in Serbo-Croatian. Nikola immediately jumped up to retrieve a blanket from his overhead luggage. I watched as the three of them stood up and draped the blanket over their legs so that it fell down to the floor, hiding the boxes behind them. On my side, Goran reached up and grabbed his duffel bag, throwing it down onto the floor in front of the box beneath him. He looked at me and looked up at my bag, silently advising me to do the same. Nikola was pulling clothes and books from his bag and creating a pile on the floor in front of him. The compartment suddenly looked like a teenage boy's bedroom. I also pulled my bag down and plopped it at my feet.

My heart was racing now. What were they smuggling? My first thought, of course, was drugs. There was that movie about the young American accused of trying to smuggle hashish out of Turkey. He was sent to a Turkish prison. But there would have to be an awful lot of hashish in those boxes for it to be hashish alone. Perhaps it was guns or some kind of explosives? I did not know about the availability of firearms in Yugoslavia, but the size of the unmarked boxes suggested that they might be carrying weapons or ammunition of some kind. I looked at the young men—they did not look like the type to be moving guns on a train from Turkey to Yugoslavia. It was most likely drugs. Hash. Maybe some opium. Or worse, it could be heroin. Shit!

A grumpy looking border policeman with sagging eyes and pendulous jowls said "Pasporti!" We handed them over, and he was quite surprised to see my little blue American document amid the familiar Yugoslav passports. He flipped it open to the first page and stared at my picture and then at me. He looked through all of my pages, raising an eyebrow. "Where you go?" he said.

"Belgrade," I said.

"You together?" He said looking at the other men in the compartment.

Before I could answer, Sasha spoke in Serbo-Croatian. Goran looked to me nervously. He smiled. He opened his box of Marlboros and offered me one. I refused. He offered them to the rest of the men, and they all began smoking again, trying to seem casual and nonplussed by the situation. The border policeman took all of our passports and left the compartment. Before his return, a customs agent entered our compartment. Sasha immediately opened his pack to offer the customs officer a cigarette. The Bulgarian gladly accepted. Goran jumped up to offer a light. The customs official spoke to Sasha. Sasha responded. I imagined that he was being asked if he had anything to declare. My heart leapt up into my esophagus. Crap. What did they have in those boxes? Sasha said something and the customs officer laughed. Sasha pointed at Nikola, speaking rapidly. The customs officer seemed amused. Sasha tossed him a pack of cigarettes. Goran fidgeted next to me.

The border police came back with our passports. He handed the others back but held on to mine. "From where are you coming?" He asked.

"Turkey," I said.

"You are alone."

"Yes," I said. "I am meeting my boyfriend in Belgrade."

"Are these men making you trouble?"

I looked around at them. They had been nothing but friendly to me despite the mysterious substance that they were smuggling. It was my chance to get out of that compartment and away from them. I could have said that I had been unable to find another free seat on the train, but this would be an obvious lie since there were many compartments with only one or two passengers in them. I thought about telling him the whole story and explaining that I had absolutely no idea what was in those unmarked boxes. But neither the customs officer nor the border policeman had yet noticed the boxes. Perhaps the best course of action was to keep my mouth shut. If I said nothing, I could pretend complete ignorance and plead that I had nothing to do with their operation should they get caught.

"No," I said, "They are students like me. We are talking about the university."

I reached into the front pocket of my rucksack and pulled out a copy of Thomas Hardy's *Return of the Native*, waving it at the border guard. He nodded in understanding. The other men in the compartment, all visibly exhaling, now started speaking to the border guard in unison. I guessed they were saying something about being students. Goran pulled out a copy of Dickens's *Oliver Twist* and flipped through the pages. Sasha sent me a furtive glance of thanks. I did not know if I was doing the right thing. I might have been getting myself into some really bad trouble. I held my breath, flipping through Hardy.

The border guard examined my passport one more time. "You have traveled a lot," he said. "You are very young."

"I am a student," I explained. "We travel to learn about the world."

"Americans," he said, slapping his hand with my passport and then giving it back to me.

He closed the door to our compartment. There was a collective sigh of relief.

"What the hell are in those . . ." I began.

"Shhh!" Said Goran. "They are not off train yet. We must wait."

"But I have the right to know what you are up to!"

"Shhhh. I explain later."

He offered me another cigarette; I refused with glaring eyes. The others all accepted and began another round in their tobacco fest. We sat in dead silence for another fifteen minutes or so. I kept staring at the blanket. What were they hiding? Would we have the same trouble all over again when we had to cross from Bulgaria into Yugoslavia? Would it be even worse? As soon as the train started moving again, and I was sure the customs officers were off the train, I would change compartments.

It seemed like forever before I felt the train begin to inch forward. I grabbed my bag and stood to leave the compartment.

"No. No. Please sit down," Goran said. Was he going to try to stop me? Was he afraid that I was going to tell someone?

"I don't know what you guys are hiding, but I don't want any trouble. I think it is best if I sit somewhere else."

Sasha also looked alarmed by the tone of my voice. He was also waving for me to sit down and said something in Serbo-Croatian.

Goran and Sasha then had a short conversation, while the other three men looked on. Goran turned to me.

"It is not what you think."

"What are you hiding in those boxes?" I said pointing to the blanket draped over their legs.

Goran looked to Sasha who nodded to Pavle who stood up and drew the curtains on the window to the door of our compartment. Sasha stood up, throwing the blanket on top of the seat. He crouched down in front of the blank box nearest to the window and carefully drew it out with both of his hands. It was heavy enough to make a slow hiss as it slid across the train floor until it was in full view. The box was rectangular and was thoroughly taped. There were no markings on it anywhere.

Sasha barked something to Pavle and Miloje who stood up to stand guard at the door. Pavle peeked out through the curtain to make sure no one was coming. He nodded back to Sasha, who reached into his pocket and pulled out a small utility knife. He carefully cut the box and pulled back the flaps.

I took a step closer, expecting that whatever was inside was probably more thoroughly packaged and still hidden from view. Instead, I saw the white tops of twelve bottles. There was something very familiar about those bottles. I leaned over to get a closer look. Sasha pulled out one of the bottles to show me what it was.

It was Heinz ketchup. They were smuggling ketchup.

"It's ketchup," I said.

"It's Heinz ketchup," Goran corrected. "We cannot get it in Yugoslavia."

"But it is just ketchup," I said, staring down at the box, a feeling of absurdity welling up inside of me. I wanted to laugh, but their behavior made it clear that the ketchup was still a dangerous contraband item. Then suddenly it hit me.

"Is ketchup illegal in communist countries?" I asked, thinking perhaps that there was a black market for ketchup in some dark alleyway in Belgrade. Perhaps there was a whole ketchup underground, running the sweetened tomato sauce into the communist world at great personal risk.

Goran looked at me as if he had not understood my question. Then he started to laugh, translating my question through hiccupping guffaws to his four friends. They started laughing too, even the cool-faced Sasha, who whacked his thigh so hard it made a loud slap. It took Goran a while to regain his composure; I was standing there between them feeling incredibly stupid. How could ketchup be illegal? Sheesh, I knew so little about the communist world.

Sasha replaced the bottle into the box, and folded the top of it closed. He slid it once more under the seat, no longer caring if the box was covered by the blanket or not. Goran explained to me that Sasha's father owned an American-style diner in Belgrade. His restaurant had become famous for serving authentic American burgers and fries, and Heinz ketchup was the key. The problem was that you could only buy bulk quantities of Heinz ketchup in Austria or Turkey, and it was much cheaper in Turkey if you were going to buy it by the case. Goran told me that the Bulgarians also produced and exported ketchup to Yugoslavia and most of the other communist countries. The Bulgarians were very proud of their ketchup and might view any claim that American ketchup tasted better as a national insult. He told me that on a previous trip to Turkey the Bulgarian customs officer had confiscated all of their ketchup, 140 bottles of it, claiming that Heinz ketchup was some form of bourgeois propaganda. In truth, Sasha believed that the Bulgarians kept it for themselves, but he never knew for sure. Now his father sends him to Turkey once a month on ketchup runs, paying the ticket for him and his friends to help him with the shipments. He did not want to lose another shipment.

I was still suspicious, but I supposed that it was plausible. It was too weird not to be. While my mind scrambled, Pavle started another cigarette round. He offered first to Sasha and then to the other men and finally he held the box at me. I took one. Goran swooped in with a lighter. I inhaled a bit, coughed a little, but then inhaled a bit more, allowing the smoke to linger in my lungs for a moment before exhaling.

The five men watched me, all smiling, all very pleased that I had finally partaken of their hospitality. I smiled back at them, twirling the cigarette between my thumb and forefinger. The Marlboro Reds were strong; I actually felt like I had a buzz.

"Good?" Sasha said in English.

"Good," I said.

Miloje opened a bag and pulled out a bottle of red wine. We had several hours left on our journey, and I had a lot to learn about life under socialism.

Eight years later, I would return to Bulgaria, and this time they gave me a thirty-day tourist visa instead of a thirty-hour transit visa. I went to visit my new boyfriend Hristo, the young Bulgarian law student from Berkeley, and to see what had happened in the eight years that had passed since my last visit to the region. Kaloyan was the first Bulgarian friend I made in Sofia. He became my friend partially because I was his best friend's American girlfriend and partially because I think he genuinely liked me. Kaloyan and Hristo had been students together in Leipzig in the late 1980s just before the wall fell. Back in Berkeley, Hristo had told me a lot of stories about Kaloyan; he was a legendary drinker and practical joker. His grandfather was one of the most important figures in Bulgaria's recent history, and he had grown up as part of the country's Communist elite. He was the Bulgarian equivalent of a Kennedy. When I first met him and his wife in March of 1998 at a little bar in Sofia called 703, I was surprised to find that he was completely without conceit. Kaloyan, his wife, Hristo, and I sat on barstools around a tall round table. They ordered rum and Cokes; I ordered a beer. My Bulgarian was still rudimentary at the time, and Kaloyan was gracious enough to speak English. His voice was low and gravelly, his accent thick, but his English was good enough to carry on a conversation for the whole evening.

He was funny and charming, with a crooked smile that was

infectious. He went out of his way to make me feel at ease, which I eventually did despite my nervousness. Kaloyan had black hair and dark brown eyes and wore jeans with a matching denim jacket. He talked with his hands, constantly waving a cigarette in the air so that his words were accompanied by swirls of smoke. He would sometimes rest a cigarette in the ashtray as he asked me a question and would then light a new one as he leaned in to listen to my reply, forgetting the first. His wife was less animated, sitting quietly and only occasionally joining in the conversation although I later learned that her English was better than his. She was an aspiring fashion designer and had her own atelier. Kaloyan was going to start his own business but had not yet decided what it would be.

During that first meeting, we talked at length about the recent economic collapse and the student protests of early 1997 that had brought down the socialist government. Bulgaria was the only communist country to democratically return their Communist leaders to power in 1990, and throughout that decade power in the country had switched back and forth between the pro-Western "democrats" and the "reformed" socialists. According to the press reports that I had read, several thousand students had spontaneously gone out into the streets to protest the faltering economy under the most recent socialist government. They filled the streets of Sofia for days, jangling their keys, metaphorically tolling the bell for the communist era. It was an impromptu demonstration like so many others throughout Eastern Europe in the months following November 1989. They did not stop their protest until the government agreed to hold early elections. Following these events, a pro-Western, pro-International Monetary Fund (IMF), and specifically pro-American government assumed power in 1997, vowing to privatize the economy and liberalize markets by implementing the structural adjustment programs of the IMF. The standard narrative was that democratic change had finally come to Bulgaria. The people had finally shaken off the chains of their communist past. The new government had a political mandate to begin restructuring the economy.

Kaloyan would have none of it.

"It was a CIA coup," he said. "Standard textbook operation. Like the one they used against Allende in 1973."

"Excuse me?" I said. I had no idea what he was talking about.

"The students were paid to demonstrate. They were given alcohol and hash and five Deutschemarks for every hour they stayed at the protests."

I looked at Hristo. He nodded his assent. I looked at Kaloyan's wife. She nodded, too.

"I never read anything about that in the newspapers," I said.

"That's because it was a covert operation," Kaloyan said. "The point was to make it look like a spontaneous demonstration."

"It wouldn't be 'covert' if you could read about it in the papers," Hristo added.

"Think about it," Kaloyan said. "In Chile they had women out on the street banging pots and pans against Allende. In Bulgaria the students were jingling their keys, ringing the bell for communism. Classic CIA tactic, something memorable for the press."

"How do you know this?" I pressed. "If this were true, someone would have figured this out by now, right?"

"Everybody knows it, but no one cares. We all wanted that government out of power."

I looked to Hristo. I never heard anything like this from him back in Berkeley, but he acted as if Kaloyan had just stated an obvious fact.

"But if everyone wanted the government out, why wouldn't they just go out and demonstrate by themselves?"

"Because Bulgarians are lazy. They don't care about anything," Kaloyan insisted. "They would never go out on the street unless someone was paying them."

"But why would the US do that?"

This time Hristo laughed at me. "Come on, Kristen, isn't that obvious?" I felt myself getting angry with him. Surely, he didn't believe all of this. Was he making fun of me?

"Bulgaria was the only country to freely reelect the Communists in 1990," Hristo continued. "We remained allies of the Soviet Union. We had a few pro-Western governments, but they never lasted. We kept reelecting socialists. We had free elections, but the Americans didn't like the outcome. It was messing up their nice little story about the 'velvet revolution.' That the people really wanted free markets and foreign investment."

"Didn't they?" I asked.

This time Hristo, Kaloyan, and his wife all laughed at me. I felt very stupid and tried to change the subject, which Kaloyan in all of his graciousness did by suggesting that we all get another round of drinks.

We went on to talk about other things, but that conversation bothered

Bulgarian-American Friendship, February 1998, in front of the National Assembly in Sofia.

me all night. It wasn't only that Kaloyan had seemed so convinced, but that Hristo had agreed with him. The following morning I asked Hristo over breakfast, "So is Kaloyan, like, big into the conspiracy theories?"

Hristo was carefully piling slabs of feta cheese and slices of tomato onto a piece of white Bulgarian bread. He lifted the open-faced sandwich to his mouth and took a bite. He chewed for a while before responding. I nibbled at some cucumbers and popped a chunk of cheese into my mouth.

"Kaloyan just doesn't believe the 'official story.' No one really does."

"But there is no proof of this, is there?"

"What kind of proof do you want? Some of the students have admitted that there was free alcohol and pot being passed around at the demonstrations. Nobody knows where it came from."

"But that doesn't prove anything."

Hristo put his sandwich down. "You don't have any proof for your version of events either."

"But all the papers say . . ."

"Do you believe everything that's printed in the papers? How do you know they are not lying?"

"Well . . ."

"You don't," he said firmly, waving a finger at me. "You just believe things because they are in print. But that doesn't make anything true."

I didn't want to get into an argument with Hristo. It was still rather early in our relationship, and we had not yet had a real fight. We'd had lots of intellectual debates about everything, from Marx's teleological theory of history to which Mexican restaurant in Berkeley made the best burrito (his favorite was Cancun, mine was Mario's), but never a fight. I could hear anger in his voice, and I did not like it.

"I don't believe everything I read," I said. I was defensive.

Hristo looked at me and sighed. "Look, Kristen, it's not your fault. You're just American. You don't understand anything."

I said nothing. He had said the word "American" as if it were an insult. It was true that I had only spent about a week in Bulgaria thus far, but I was not some garden-variety stupid American who had never been anywhere outside of the country. I had traveled around Europe and the Middle East by myself for a year when I was only nineteen. I had been a junior exchange student for nine months in Ghana and had lived for three years in Japan between undergraduate and graduate school. In fact, I'd been in a hell of a lot more countries than he'd ever been in. I bit my tongue for a moment more, but then I could not help myself. "Actually, I understand quite a few things," I said. "And this sounds like some crazy conspiracy theory bullshit to me."

Hristo froze. My anger surprised him. He put his hand on mine and said, "I mean you don't understand anything about Bulgaria. About what it's like here. Sometimes the conspiracy theories are true."

"Give me one example," I said, pulling my hand away to take a sip of coffee.

"Chernobyl," he said as if he was definitively closing the subject.

"What do you mean? The nuclear accident in Ukraine? Everybody knew about Chernobyl. It exploded. That's no secret. Or are you going to tell me that the CIA is responsible for that, too?"

"Everybody in the West knew," Hristo said. His voice changed. It became softer. "But nobody told us."

"What do you mean?" I asked, letting my anger dissipate. There were probably a lot of things that I did not know about Bulgaria.

"When it happened the government tried to cover it up. They didn't tell anybody. It was not in the newspapers or on the news. You know I was in

A group of Bulgarian
draftees, circa 1986.

the army at the time, and my mom was working for the Central Committee.
I got this weird call from her, and she told me not to eat any vegetables,
especially lettuce. It was late April, and that is the time when all Bulgarians
eat green salad to celebrate the arrival of spring. It's all lettuce and green
onions and carrots. Everybody eats it for Easter, you know."

"Why not lettuce?" I asked.

"Because it was irradiated. It would make us sick. I mean, really sick.
Lettuce is a water intensive crop and all of the radiation from Chernobyl
was coming into Bulgaria in the rain."

"Oh my God . . ."

"Yeah, and the government didn't say anything. A few people really high
up in the Communist Party knew about it and somehow my mom found
out. I don't know if she knew what happened, but someone told her not to

eat vegetables and she figured out that there was something very wrong going on.

"You know, I was in a mobile missile unit at the time and we had these handheld Geiger counters. So I started testing the supply crates of vegetables because I suspected that it had something to do with radiation. Because it wasn't cucumbers from Shumen or grapes from Haskovo, it was all vegetables from all of Bulgaria, which meant it wasn't some local chemical spill. It had to be radiation. I told the other guys in my unit, but no one believed me. They thought I was paranoid. That I was nuts. The officer in charge even put me on latrine duty for spreading false rumors. He told everyone in the unit that if there had been a nuclear accident that the government would have mobilized the army to assist in a cleanup operation. He said the government would have issued public safety announcements about what vegetables were safe to eat."

Hristo paused here. I could see that he was quite upset.

"For a while I began to doubt it too. I thought my mom was crazy. Some of the guys in the unit would heap piles of salad on their plates just to show me that they thought I was an asshole. But my mom called me again, and she sounded really scared. She told me not to eat the lettuce. She said that she was not supposed to tell anyone, that no one was supposed to know, but she was worried about me. I told her about the guys in my unit, and she said it was understandable that they wouldn't believe me. She said it didn't matter what they thought. She wanted me to be safe.

"You know, Kristen, I was only nineteen, and I didn't know what to believe. But my parents were pretty high up in the party and if there was a big secret or something, they might be in a position to know about it."

I looked across the table at him and imagined him as a nineteen-year-old in the army. He would actually become a lieutenant in the Bulgarian military, and years later when he applied for his American green card he would have to answer yes to the questions about whether he had ever been a member of the Communist Party or served in the armed forces of a foreign nation. The frustration in his voice was palpable even though he was describing events that had happened over a decade earlier. I nodded for him to continue.

"They all laughed at me for a while. My commanding officer gave me a lot of shit. But then some people in Bulgaria heard from the BBC and the

A Bulgarian soldier, circa 1986.

VOA that there had been a nuclear accident in the USSR and that there was irradiated rain falling in Western Europe. In those days it was illegal to listen to the Western radio stations, the BBC World Service, and the Voice of America, but a lot of Bulgarians did anyway. They could have been arrested if they were caught, but lots took the risk just to hear about what was really going on. And once people heard it on the Western radio, everyone started asking questions. The higher-ups tried to tell us that it was all American disinformation, but I knew better. Eventually the government had to admit what had happened, but only after millions of people had eaten the contaminated vegetables.

"And you know the funny thing. Those guys in my unit who had eaten all that lettuce, they were scared shitless when they found out the truth. But they never said they were sorry to me. They just hated me even more because they knew my parents had privileges that theirs didn't and that's why I knew about it."

A group of high school girls at military camp in 1987.

"But you tried to warn them . . ."

"It didn't matter. A lot of people really believed in communism, they could not believe that the government would do something so much against the people. Rather than blaming the system, they wanted to blame the leaders. Bulgarians learned then to be skeptical of any official story. That's why Kaloyan and I are the way we are. That's why no one believes about the demonstrations . . ."

"But that was communism," I interrupted. "This is democracy."

Hristo folded his hands and looked me straight in the eye, shaking his head from side to side. "Do you really think there is any difference?"

When she said that communism ruined her life, I knew that she meant it. It was 1999, and I was doing interviews with women working in the tourism industry. Many of the women I interviewed thus far were inclined to look back on the era before 1989 as a time of relative order and prosperity compared to the mafia-infested present. But Damiana had a very different story to tell.

When I met her she was the marketing manager for one of the biggest hotels in Borovetz, a ski resort just outside of Sofia. The resort had been one of the crown jewels of Balkantourist, the state-run tourism enterprise that owned and operated all of Bulgaria's tourism infrastructure. After 1989 Balkantourist was broken up into smaller pieces and privatized even though it was still generating revenue for the state. Privatization was the process of taking enterprises that had been previously owned and operated by the government (like the United States Postal Service) and selling them off to individuals or privately owned companies. Under communism there had been almost no private sector; all industries, services, and agricultural units were state owned and often subsidized if they started to lose money. The subsidies were always justified as a way to keep people fully employed. Unlike Bulgaria's heavy industries that were constantly in need of money from the state budget, however, tourism had always been solvent. The privatization of the tourism industry was ideologically driven. In a free market economy the state should not own enterprises, even in cases where the state was managing to do a reasonable job.

Borovetz was one of the first resorts to be broken up and privatized. Its hotels and restaurants had been sold to a new class of criminal elites, thugs, and corrupt politicians. Employees were not receiving their wages on time, and guests were unhappy with the deteriorating quality of service. Given this situation, most of Damiana's colleagues in the resort had very mixed feelings about the coming of democracy. But Damiana was unequivocal. Communism was evil. Communism had ruined her life.

From my vantage point sitting across her large wooden desk, her life certainly did not appear to be ruined. Damiana sat comfortably in a large, swivel chair behind a newish looking computer screen. She told me that she was forty-five years old, but she did not look a day over forty. She was a broad-boned woman a little on the heavy side, but she had a remarkably smooth and serene face with only a few telling wrinkles around her eyes and two shallow indentations running from the corners of her nose to the edges of her mouth. Her green eyes were wide and almond shaped, set perfectly under the impeccably groomed arcs of her eyebrows. Her hair was brown, and she wore it in a pageboy hairstyle just long enough to brush the tops of her shoulders. Damiana wore a neatly pressed blue suit. I caught sight of ten manicured fingernails when she waved her hands as she spoke. Overall, she gave the impression of a woman who had once been stunningly beautiful and was aging with dignity and self-confidence.

It was the first time I had interviewed her, but I had asked her permission to interview the other employees in the hotel. I knew that she approved of my project. She had also given me the names of colleagues in other hotels. I was quite sure she had heard about my interviews with them. After several weeks, she finally found some time to sit down and speak with me about the inner workings of Borovetz. The first hour of the interview had been spent talking about the complications of running a private hotel and the changes that privatization had required of the old Communist hotel managers.

"So could you tell me a little about how you started working in tourism?" I asked. "Your educational background. Your previous work experience. Additional training or special courses that you might have taken."

"I was young when I first started working in tourism," she told me in flawless English. "I always knew I wanted to work in a resort, and I went to an English-language secondary school so that I would be prepared for the tourism entrance exams. I earned my tourism degree from the geography department at Sofia University and was sent to the seaside to do my national service in the Golden Sands Resort."

Before 1989, the government had guaranteed free university education to all Bulgarians who chose to pursue advanced degrees, but competition for the most desirable subjects was fierce. Entrance into preparatory secondary schools was based on student performance on difficult exams designed to sort youth into different professions. Because the Bulgarian government also guaranteed full employment to all citizens, the education system was designed to produce only as many graduates as the economy needed. Rather than accepting more students than there would ultimately be jobs for, universities in centrally planned economies theoretically only produced the number of graduates required to fill the expected needs of predetermined five-year plans.

Upon graduation from a particular department at the university, the government also guaranteed all young Bulgarians a job in their chosen field for two or three years. These positions were chosen by the state, however, and young graduates were the most likely to be sent where no one else wanted to go. For Damiana to have graduated from tourism (one of the most competitive departments to get into) at Sofia University (the most prestigious university in the country) and then be sent to Golden Sands (one of the two premier summer resorts in Bulgaria) right after graduation was a sign that she was incredibly smart and came from a politically well-connected family. Damiana had been one of the privileged ones under the old system, a member of the post-1989 cohort most likely to look back with fondness on the totalitarian era. What could have happened to her, I wondered, as she continued telling me about her career trajectory in the tourism industry.

"After my three years in Golden Sands, I decided that I wanted to stay on the seaside and become a hotel manager. I was twenty-eight and still unmarried at the time. You know, women in Bulgaria tend to marry early. I had some boyfriends, but nothing serious. I wanted to be a manager and was not ready to have children. But I suppose it was because I had never really fallen in love. You know, really in love."

I nodded to her, scribbling notes as we spoke. Her voice seemed to change when she said the word *love*. It got thicker and the words came more slowly.

"I was sent on a friendship exchange to Cuba in the winter of 1983, to learn about our brother socialist country and as a reward for being a good worker in the resort. I was also studying Spanish as my fifth language."

"Your fifth?"

She smiled. "Well, I could speak Bulgarian, Russian, and English from secondary school. And then I studied French at university. So Spanish was my fifth."

"And so you went to Cuba for language training?"

"Not officially for the language. More like a tour. But I spent all of the time there practicing Spanish. And that is where I met Manuel."

She spoke his name like the first note of a song. I nodded for her to continue.

"Well," she said. "I was still young. He was studying to become a doctor, a pediatrician. At the University of Havana. And he was so handsome. Like a dark prince."

She paused. Her voice had started to quiver, and I could see that her eyes were glassy with a threatening shower of tears. At this point, I stopped writing down her words, feeling that she wanted me to give her my full attention. I was a stranger, and she was going to tell me something very personal.

The story went something like this. She spent a winter with Manuel in Havana, and they fell deeply in love with each other. Manuel was a consummate Cuban patriot, sharing with her every corner of his beloved city. Damiana fell in love with the country as much as she had fallen in love with the man, soaking in the successes of Cuban socialism. Damiana met Manuel's parents and sisters and had been welcomed as a member of their family when she could get away from the other Bulgarians in her group. She was twenty-eight and was in love for the first time in her life. It was with bitter despair that she boarded the plane back to Sofia in late March.

Biweekly letters ensued with Manuel pouring out pages and pages of Spanish prose telling Damiana how much he loved her and begging her to return to Havana. In early May, she found out she was pregnant but decided that she would have an abortion, fearing that it was too soon in their relationship for a child. She was also desperate to make sure that she would be allowed to return to Cuba the following winter.

She spent the next nine months working in the resort and continuing to practice her Spanish. With five languages and five years experience, Damiana was given a promotion to become the manager of the reception desk in the most luxurious hotel on the seaside. It was a big honor for someone so young and surely meant that she would be managing her own hotel in the not too distant future. She applied for and was granted another exit visa to go to Cuba the following winter. This time, she did not even bother to stay with the other Bulgarians on the friendship tour. Damiana stayed at Manuel's parents' house, and they began to make plans to get married as soon as Manuel finished his studies at the university.

It was March of 1984 when Damiana returned to Bulgaria to announce to her parents that she was engaged and planning to immigrate to Cuba. Stunned, her parents tried to dissuade her at first but then relented. Damiana was quite old by Bulgarian standards and even though they would miss her terribly, they both realized it might be her last chance to find happiness. She would have to get permission from the state authorities. It would also mean quitting her job and giving up her dream to be a hotel manager. Damiana did not care. She had finally found love. She was not going to let it go.

"I wrote to him every day. I wrote to him in Spanish about the life we were going to build together. About the house we might someday have. About our future children. What we would call them. He wanted the boys to have Spanish names like Raul and Pedro. I preferred Bulgarian names like Ivan or Dimitar. But we both agreed that our first daughter would be named Maria, because it is a girl's name in both Spanish and Bulgarian. And his father's mother was Maria. And if we had a second daughter, she would be named Anna, which also works in both languages. But we quarreled over the boys' names. We quarreled over the names of children we did not yet have!" she laughed.

The last letter she received from Manuel was on November 13, 1984.

"Sometimes there was a week or two between his letters, but they always came. I never had to wait for more than a few weeks. I started to worry when a month went by. Then two months. At that point, I was writing him every day. Then three months went by. I spent Christmas and New Year's

Eve with my parents in Sofia, not leaving the house. Back then it was very expensive to make international calls, and you had to go through a telephone operator who dialed the number for you."

The international operators in Bulgaria were all informants for the state security services. International calls could not be placed without government permission.

"I tried to call him at his parents' house," she continued, "but the operator told me that the number did not exist anymore. I applied for an exit visa to return to Cuba. It was denied. He was not writing. I could not call him. There was no way I could leave to go see him."

Her voice was low and filled with rage and disappointment.

"I was a prisoner in my own country. After two years of receiving letters from him almost every week the silence was terrible. I did not know what to think. Was he still alive? Surely, his parents would have written to tell me. They loved me. Had he met someone else? Maybe, but I know he would have told me; he would have tried to explain. That was his way, to be honest. I knew he would not just stop loving me, even if he fell in love with someone else. I could not understand what happened."

Damiana applied for an exit visa to go to Cuba several more times but was denied. She was told that she was needed to work in Borovetz and could not be spared in the winter months. She tried to call his home in Havana, but she was always told by the Bulgarian operator that the number did not exist. She wrote him letters every week but never received a reply. Her parents tried to convince her that he had abandoned her; that she should get on with her life. Everything in Damiana's world seemed to come crashing down around her. She stopped eating and had to be hospitalized for two weeks.

"I loved him. I could not just stop loving him. You cannot turn your heart off like an air conditioner," she told me.

She read and reread all of his letters searching for some clue as to why he had disappeared. For five years she worked in the Borovetz resort hoping and waiting. Her fantasy was that someday Manuel would walk through the front doors of the hotel. But he never came. She never heard from him again. There was only silence.

Damiana was thirty-five when communism fell. She had never married. She had no children. She often thought of the child she might have had if she had not terminated the pregnancy.

"At least then I would have had a part of him. A little Maria or Pedro who would remind me that it had been real. That it was not all a dream."

She thought about going to Cuba to find him but decided against it. She could not find the time to get away. The years had passed, Damiana had risen through the ranks, and by 1998 Damiana was one step away from managing the biggest hotel in Borovetz. She had tried his phone number in Havana one last time, free of the intrusive Bulgarian operator, but after over a decade she was not surprised to find that it was indeed out of service. She wrote one more letter to his parents' house in Havana. Time had squashed whatever hope she had left.

One day she received a telephone call from her mother. A large box had been delivered to their house in Sofia with Damiana's name on it. She took a bus into Sofia that night.

Since 1997 Bulgaria had been ruled by a coalition of pro-Western democratic parties under the leadership of Prime Minister Ivan Kostov. The Kostov administration was virulently anticommunist, and for a brief time the government gave access to the communist-era dossiers of about twenty-five thousand Bulgarian citizens. Under communism, the state security services kept a close watch on individual citizens, compiling files on anyone who was potentially considered a threat to the regime. Through a vast network of informants, the state security services could keep tabs on everyone, with children sometimes spying on their own parents and parents on their own children. Those who worked in tourism were particularly watched because they had regular access to Westerners. Damiana always knew that there were state security agents in the resorts, but she was quite sure that they had no interest in her. She did not care that she was being watched or that her employees were informing on her actions. Damiana never believed that she had anything to hide.

That night when she returned to Sofia, her mother met her at the door with the box. "I knew," she said, "but I could not tell you. I was not sure what they might do to us. What they might do to you."

Damiana was confused, but could tell by the tears in her mother's eyes that it was something quite serious.

"Your father requested your file last year," her mother continued. "We thought you had the right to know. Now that it is safe."

Damiana opened the box. Inside was her state security dossier, which included a stack of about 250 opened letters stapled to their envelopes. She recognized her own handwriting on about half of them. The other letters were all his. There were over 150 letters from Manuel that Damiana had never seen. The first three or four were sent from Havana. The rest were all sent from Miami.

Manuel had defected to the United States.

From the early letters it seems that he was trying to tell her of his plans in code. Something had happened to his father, making it necessary for the whole family to leave Havana. He was going to have to quit medical school and go with them. He did not want to leave but could not stay behind. The letters seemed nervous and hurried, but Manuel ended each letter with a wish that he and Damiana would be together soon. He wanted nothing more than to marry her and spend the rest of his life with her. He could not stand to be separated from her, and he feared that she might not want to come to Cuba if he was not "living in Havana."

There was a long time gap between the last of the letters from Cuba and the first of the letters from the United States. Manuel knew it was dangerous to write to her, but he wanted to explain what had happened. Even though he knew that it would be almost impossible for them to be together, he felt compelled to tell her that he still loved her. If she could send him some word, he would try to come to Bulgaria to find her. But he was also afraid that his letters would cause problems for her and her family. He agonized about writing them but said he could not help himself.

In letter after letter, written over four years, Manuel hoped that Damiana would wait for him; that she did not hate him for defecting, because it was not his decision; that they would find a way to be together. "Please write to me," he wrote, "if only to tell me that you never want to hear from me again."

But none of their letters ever reached each other. Once the Bulgarian secret services realized that Manuel had defected, they suspected that Damiana had known about his plan all along and was planning to defect as well. The state security police had put Damiana under close surveillance, and all of Manuel and Damiana's letters were intercepted and analyzed for clues about her plans to escape Bulgaria. Her multiple applications for exit visas confirmed their suspicions, and it was suggested that she be removed from her job in the resort. It was only the personal connections of her parents, who had been interrogated by the state security, which saved her. They insisted to important superiors in the Ministry of the Interior that

Damiana knew nothing about the defection. Her parents argued that she was a naïve and heartbroken woman who was now too old to marry. It would be unnecessarily cruel for the government to deprive her of her profession when she had done nothing but fall in love with the "wrong" sort of man. A few carefully placed bribes did the trick.

After fifteen years of anguish, Damiana told me that it took her only a few hours to read through all of his letters. The later ones seemed more and more resigned, as he began to lose hope of ever seeing her again. The last letter in the pile was postmarked September 7, 1989. He wrote to tell her that he could not wait for her any longer. He was getting married to a woman who was expecting his child. He was sorry and hoped that she would find happiness in her life.

She opened the top drawer of her desk and took out a creased airmail envelope. "I still keep the letter with me. It was September. Just two months before the wall fell. I could have gone to stop him. If he had just waited two months more, we could have been together."

She gently placed the letter on her desk, smoothing it out with two hands, caressing it. I looked down at the envelope, deeply moved by her story. Maybe an hour had passed since she started the tale, and I was so wrapped up in her world that I forgot myself and blurted out, "But you have spoken to him since, right? You've gotten back in touch now that it is possible?"

She shook her head. No.

I looked down at the envelope and saw the small letters written in the upper left hand side: sw 15th Street, Coral Terrace, FL 33144.

"But you have his address. You could write him a letter!"

Damiana sighed. "Yes, I have often thought so, too. I've spent the last year thinking about it. But he is now married with a child. What would I say in a letter? What is there to gain but more suffering?"

"This letter is from ten years ago. What if he got divorced? Do you know what the divorce rate is in the United States?"

At this, Damiana looked at me as if she was seeing me for the first time.

"You are an American," she said.

"Yes," I said.

"What I would really like to do is call him. It would feel more correct than trying to write a letter that might get lost or that his wife might throw away."

"Do you know his phone number?"

"No." She looked at me. "Do you know how to find it?"

This was late 1999 and the Internet was still a relatively new thing in the world, especially in Bulgaria. Google was only a year old, and most of us still relied on Yahoo or Netscape search engines for finding information on the Web, of which there was still a very limited amount. It was worth a try.

"Do you have Internet?" I asked.

"Yes."

"Well, it is a long shot, but there is Yahoo People Search."

"Do I have that on my computer?" She asked.

I walked around to her side of the desk and leaned over her monitor. "If you have Internet, we should be able to access it. Do you have dial-up or an Ethernet connection?"

"I don't know," she said. "I just turn it on."

"Probably Ethernet then," I said, typing in the URL "people.yahoo.com" into her Internet Explorer window. "What is his name?"

"Manuel Fernandez."

"Hmmm. That is a really common name. Especially in Miami. And if he has moved in the last ten years, he will be impossible to find."

I typed in his name and the zip code from the envelope. "This probably isn't going to work. But let's see." I did not want to get her hopes up.

I clicked the search button. The computer starting processing. I heard Damiana take in a sharp breath and hold it. She clutched the letter in her right hand, making a nervous fist with her left. The computer was slow. I began to suspect that maybe she did have a dial up connection. As the computer thought, Damiana exhaled.

"This is a waste of time," she said. "What would I say to him now? I don't even remember much Spanish anymore."

"He probably speaks English," I offered, hopefully.

The computer stopped thinking.

Manuel Fernandez. sw 15th Street, Coral Terrace, Florida 33144. And a phone number.

"I think we found him," I said. I was really surprised. It seemed like such a long shot to me, but as I stared at the screen and the address on the envelope from his last letter I was quite sure that this was the right person. "And here is his phone number."

"That is all it took? You just had to type in his name?"

"Well, it helped that you had the address."

"You mean I could have done this last year?"

"Probably," I said.

Her face went pale. "It was there all this time?"

"It is hard to know when the information was put on the Web," I said. "But the Internet is incredible."

I sat staring at the screen.

"What time is it in the States?" Damiana whispered.

I looked at the clock. It was 4:13 p.m. in Bulgaria, which meant it was morning on the East Coast. And it was Saturday.

"You could probably call him right now," I said.

Her eyes widened. "No," she said. "I can't. It is too late for all of that now."

Doing ethnography is a funny thing. There I was in a room with a woman I hardly knew, and all I could think about was this man in Miami that had defected and waited for her for five years but had given up hope just months before she would have been able to join him there. I had this strong mental image of Damiana, this beautiful and poised woman beside me, convulsing with tears as she read through the letters the state security services had kept from her for all those years. Here was a chance to set things right, to undo the sad Cold War tragedy that was this woman's life. Maybe I had an incurable romantic streak, but I could not help myself. I wanted them to speak, for her to find out that he was divorced and that he was still in love with him. For him to get on a plane and come to Bulgaria tomorrow so that they could be reunited at last. It seemed totally crazy, but his phone number was sitting on the screen in front of me.

"Can you make international calls from here?" I asked, pointing at the phone on her desk.

She nodded.

"If you want, I could call the number for you. Just to make sure that it is him."

She stared at me.

"You know, I could just call and ask for Manuel to see if a woman answers the phone or something. I have an American accent, and I can pretend that it's a wrong number or something. I don't mind doing it. Just to be sure that it is him."

"What will you say?"

"I don't know. Whatever you want me to say. If a woman answers the phone, I could just hang up."

I laughed for a moment. Here I was in Bulgaria with a forty-five-year-old woman planning a prank phone call to the United States.

"What harm can it do?" I said. "At least you will know if it is the right number."

"Okay," she said. "You will have to dial two zeros to get an international line."

I picked up the phone and started to dial. I pushed two zeros and a one and then hung up.

I turned to Damiana. "What do you want me to do if he answers the phone?"

She bit her lip.

"Do you want to talk to him?"

"No. Well, maybe. Yes. I suppose if he answers the phone . . ."

"Okay?" I said, interrupting her.

"Okay."

I dialed the number. I heard the familiar sound of an American telephone ring. In Europe the ring of the telephone is different, two short rings rather than one long one. After the fifth ring, I got an automated recording: "We're sorry, the number you have dialed is disconnected or is no longer in service. If you feel you have reached this recording in error, please hang up and try your call again."

No! I thought to myself. It cannot be. He has to be there.

"What happened?" Damiana asked, her brow furrowed with concern.

"I think I must have dialed the wrong number. Let me try again."

I dialed the two zeros for the international line, the one for the United States, the area code for Coral Terrace, and the seven digits of the phone number from Yahoo People Search. The phone rang once. Twice. Three times. Four times.

"Hello?"

"Hello? May I please speak to Manuel Fernandez?"

"Speaking."

I gulped. "Um. I am sorry to bother you, but I am trying to track down an old friend with your same name. He left Cuba in 1984."

"Who is this?"

"Um. I am . . . um . . . I am a friend of . . . I am calling from Bulgaria."

"Bulgaria?" The voice on the phone had been aggressive, almost annoyed. Now it seemed softer. It was him!

"Yes, Bulgaria. I am calling on behalf of a friend." I looked over to Damiana whose face was now the color of newly fallen snow. I nodded to her, pointing to the phone. She shook her head back at me, clearly aghast that I might actually be talking to *her* Manuel.

"Who is this?" the voice demanded.

"My . . . my name is Kristen. I am a friend of Damiana's. In Bulgaria . . ."

"Damiana?" His voice cracked. "Is she alive?"

"Actually," I said, staring at the woman beside me, "she is right here. Would you like to speak with her?"

There was a very long silence on the other end.

"I mean, is now a good time? Would it be better for her to call you later?"

"Damiana . . ." the voice said.

"I'll put her on," I said. I offered the phone to Damiana. I could tell by her face that she was totally shocked. I motioned for her to take the phone. She hesitated.

"Damiana, it's him. It's really him."

She very slowly took the phone from my hands and lifted it to her ear.

"Manuel?" she said, still staring at me.

I could not hear his reply, but Damiana's cheeks were soon streaked with tears as she listened, cradling the phone with two hands against her cheek. I walked around to the other side of her desk, quickly gathering up my notebook and purse so that I could give her some privacy. I waved a hasty good-bye. Damiana smiled at me through her tears as I closed the door behind me, walking out into the cool, wide lobby. I walked out of the hotel and took a deep breath of the fresh mountain air.

It was going to be a very nice evening.

CHAPTER 4   **HAIR**

Yordanka saw the sign as she walked to the pharmacy to buy her father's medicine. It was just a photocopied piece of white paper pasted to a lamppost. At first she thought it was an obituary, a Xeroxed A4 flyer announcing the death of a local resident. These were ubiquitous in her small, depopulated city that was now inhabited primarily by pensioners. But the sign said in big, bold block Cyrillic letters: "We buy Hair. Up to 100 leva for long, healthy hair."

Yordanka instinctively reached up and fingered one of the curls spilling down over her shoulders. She had the kind of hair that always made other girls jealous. It was thick, dark, and shiny, falling in a cascade of cylindrical springs all the way to her lower back. Yordanka had an average face and was a little on the heavy side for a girl of her height, but no one ever seemed to notice those things. She was considered beautiful because she had beautiful hair. She was very proud of it; washing and conditioning it with olive oil as often as she could.

Yordanka was a Bulgarian Muslim, and although her father had become increasingly religious in his old age, he never dreamed of asking her to wear a headscarf because he knew how vain she was about her hair. In recent years many Muslims became newly convinced that it was immodest for women to walk around in public with their heads uncovered, although there were still plenty of

Xeroxed obituaries are often posted around the neighborhood of the recently deceased.

young Muslim women like Yordanka who rejected this idea. She pushed some tendrils behind her right ear and marched toward the pharmacy. No one could ever make her cover up or cut her hair. But one hundred leva was a lot of money. And she had no job.

They're buying hair in Muslim villages, Yordanka thought, because we are poor and because they think we don't care about being pretty. But Yordanka knew better. So many of her supposedly modest friends were total sluts behind closed doors, having sex indiscriminately with both Muslim and Christian boys alike. A lot of those girls wore the headscarf to please their parents, knowing that they could stay out later and be more independent if their parents thought they were appropriately dressed. Yordanka had also heard rumors that the local imam paid some girls to cover their heads to set an example to others. But she had never been able to find out if this was really true. What she did know was that some of the girls were real fanatics. They actually believed in God and the Qur'an and didn't eat pork or drink beer. Why, she thought, would God care what she ate or didn't eat? If there really was a God, Yordanka was sure that he had far more important things to do.

She walked into the pharmacy. "Good day," she said.

"Good day," said the pharmacist.

"I am here to pick up my father's medicine."

"Ah yes, Todorov, Alexander, correct?"

"Yes, it was a special order."

"Oh yes, I remember it. It came from Plovdiv yesterday. Quite expensive, if I recall."

Yordanka swallowed. This was not what she wanted to hear. She had left the house with twenty leva, the last money they had. She thought the medicine would cost no more than ten leva and that she would still have ten leva left for food. If she did not buy meat, she could buy enough potatoes, onions, carrots, lentils, and rice to last them a week, including a loaf of fresh bread and maybe a little olive oil for her hair. They could get milk and yogurt from her aunt in the village. Her father made homemade brandy with wild plums. With just ten leva, they would have been fine for another seven days until her father's pension payment came.

"How much is it?"

The pharmacist rifled through a box of white bags and pulled one out. Yordanka felt her heart beating.

"Here it is. Thirty-two leva."

"Thirty-two leva? But my father is a pensioner."

"Yes, dear, but . . ."

"And he only gets 210 leva a month."

"Well, this is a month's supply."

"How can we afford thirty-two leva a month? We can barely eat on the money we have now."

"I am sorry, but this medication is not on the formulary."

"Why would the doctor prescribe it?"

"Because, my dear," the middle-aged pharmacist said gently, "it is the medicine your father needs to get well."

Yordanka looked at the pharmacist, a woman in her fifties with a pudgy but kind face. She wore a white uniform coat over a plain gray dress with black piping around the hem and the ends of the sleeves. Her gray-blond hair was neatly piled away into a knot at the back of her head, and she wore a simple beaded necklace around the loose skin of her neck. Yordanka did not have enough money and wanted to plead with the woman, but she thought better of it. She was sure the pharmacist had heard it all before.

Madan was a very poor town of old sick people who needed all sorts of medicines.

Yordanka knew that this pharmacist was a fair woman who never cheated or tried to take advantage of other people's misery, unlike the other pharmacist near the hospital. That pharmacist, from the nearby city of Zlatograd, had paid a bribe to open a shop right in front of the main entrance of the hospital. He charged at least three leva on top of every prescription, claiming that his rent was very high. But everyone in town knew that he drove an Audi from Zlatograd to Madan every morning. He was an outsider, a Christian, and he was not to be trusted. But his pharmacy was very conveniently located, and he kept a lot more medicine in stock than this one did.

The pharmacist standing behind the counter was a Muslim who had lived in Madan all her life. She did not own a car. Many people knew and respected her. She did not inflate prices. Medicine was just expensive.

"I only have twenty leva," Yordanka sighed.

The pharmacist sighed back. "You're little Yordanka Todorova, right?"

Yordanka nodded.

"I knew your mother. A very good woman. I was very sorry to hear . . ."

The voice of the pharmacist trailed off. Yordanka's mother had died two years earlier. She was only forty-six years old. It was an aneurism, completely unexpected. She had been in perfect health before that. Yordanka was just starting her senior year of secondary school, considering where she might apply to university. She was very good at German and hoped to study philology, but after her mother's unexpected death she gave up any hope of leaving Madan. She was an only child, and her father was already ill. He took his wife's death very hard; they had been married for twenty-five years.

In Yordanka's entire life she had never seen her father cry. But when they left the hospital the night her mother passed away, her father had come home and poured himself one very tall glass of Bulgarian brandy without even offering the bottle to Yordanka. It was only when he put the cup to his lips that Yordanka realized how hard his hands were shaking. She stood there in the doorway of the very small kitchen where her mother had spent the last eighteen years cooking for them. She watched her father drain his glass in a series of frantic gulps—his Adam's apple bobbing up and down as he drank.

Yordanka's father eventually put the glass down. He stared at the refrigerator. His eyes did not seem to blink or move. He just kept staring.

"Daddy," Yordanka had said. He did not reply. He just stared.

It was maybe an hour that Yordanka stood watching her father from the doorway, swallowing her own grief so as not to cause him any more pain.

Then he started crying. Quietly at first, a few tears rolling silently down his tanned and weathered cheeks. And then it was violent. He let out a long anguished groan, and the tears flowed down and mixed with the mucus that was running out of his nostrils, down into his mouth where it mixed with saliva, and then it dripped down his chin and onto the front of his shirt, which was soaked through in a matter of moments. He did not bother to wipe his face. He did not pour himself a second glass of brandy. He just moaned and rocked back and forth in his chair saying nothing.

Yordanka realized that she could not leave him.

"I knew your mother well, actually," said the pharmacist, interrupting Yordanka's memory of that horrible day. "She was a classmate of my younger sister and used to come to our house when they were in grade school."

Yordanka's mouth twitched into a slight smile as she imagined her mother as a young girl going to a friend's house to play.

"I have already ordered this medicine, and I won't be able to sell it to anyone else," said the pharmacist leaning over the counter and gazing at Yordanka. "You can give me the twenty leva today and pay me the other twelve when you have the money. I know how hard things have been for you and your father, but I insist on being paid. I cannot run a pharmacy by giving medicine away. I have to pay for this medicine with my own money."

Yordanka nodded, opening her mouth to say thank you.

"No need to thank me. I have to stay in business or else no one in Madan will have medicine. Two pharmacies have already closed, and do you know why? Because people here blame the pharmacist if their medicine is too expensive. But we have nothing to do with this! The doctors prescribe, the private companies set the prices, and we only fill orders. No one wants to take advantage of sick people, but how are we to run a business if we can't charge at least what we ourselves have paid, plus a little extra so that we can live?"

Yordanka said nothing.

"If I closed my pharmacy," the woman said, "there would only be one pharmacy left in Madan, and then he would raise his prices."

"Everyone knows you are an honest woman," Yordanka finally said. "We know that you are good. It's just that it is so hard."

"Yes. I know," said the pharmacist. "It is hard for all of us now. It was much better when the government made the drugs. They say the drugs are safer now, but I know there was nothing wrong with the old ones. I was a pharmacist for twenty years, and I tell you that the medicines were just fine."

"I will pay you the money as soon as my father gets his next pension payment," Yordanka interrupted her.

"I know you will, my dear. You are a good girl, just like your poor mother."

The pharmacist took out a slip of paper and made a note saying that Yordanka Todorova owed the pharmacy twelve leva and asked Yordanka to sign it.

"The best thing to do now," advised the pharmacist, slipping the signed piece of paper into her drawer, "is to go to your father's doctor and ask if there is a medication that is on the formulary. It may not be exactly what he needs, but if there is something close it will be much cheaper."

Yordanka nodded. She would definitely go to see her father's doctor. "Thank you so much," she said. "I will pay you as soon as I can." She gave the pharmacist the twenty leva bill and took the white bag with her father's medication in it. She hoped it would make him better. She was now twenty-one years old, but she did not want to be an orphan just yet. She walked out of the pharmacy into the bright sunshine and reached up to twirl a tendril of her long hair around her pointer finger.

They were now completely broke. Yordanka walked past the ATM where she would withdraw her father's 210 leva pension payment in a week. The truth was that it was her mother that had kept the family going after 1989. During the communist era, they had been quite well off because her father worked for the big lead and zinc mining enterprise. Although Yordanka had often wished for Western jeans or other consumer items, she had never experienced any real deprivation in Madan until the 1990s. Thankfully, they were able to manage for a while because Yordanka's mother had been a seamstress and was able to maintain her position in the garment factory after it was privatized to an Austrian company. She could sew well, and she could sew fast. Since all of the employees were paid on a piece rate, Yordanka's mother had been able to earn almost five hundred leva a month depending on the pattern they were sewing.

Her father, on the other hand, had worked as a machinist in a factory that was a key production unit of the mining industry. Like so many other men in the city, he had not been able to find new work when the mining enterprise was privatized and run into bankruptcy. Yordanka's father spent his free time helping to build the new mosque that was being constructed in the center of the city. As part of the Communists' desire to eradicate all religious belief, they had bulldozed the old mosque in the late 1950s to make room for the administrative offices of the massive lead and zinc mining enterprise. After 1989, when the mines eventually closed, there were a lot of men with little to do. The building of the new mosque gave them a reason to get up in the morning. But it paid nothing. Yordanka's father was unemployed for years before his illness. He had already been home on a disability pension for two years before his wife's death.

After just barely graduating from secondary school, Yordanka stayed home with her father for the summer to keep him company and nurse her own grief. She soon realized that they would not be able to live on her father's disability pension alone. She would have to get a job. She tried to find something in Madan. The few jobs for shopkeepers paid little, and the owners preferred to hire their own relatives and friends. Although her mother had tried to teach her, Yordanka had no talent for sewing. For a while, she tried commuting every day to Smolyan, the nearest big city, to work in a café as a waitress. But the bus fare back and forth to Madan ate up a big portion of her wages, and Yordanka wasted two hours a day in travel time. He father was usually asleep in the morning when she left and asleep in the evening when she returned.

"Why don't you go to Sofia?" He had asked her one early June Saturday when she was home.

"But Sofia is so far," she said. Secretly, she would have loved to get out of Madan and live in the capital for a while. She knew that the wages there were much higher, and she longed for the company of other young people her own age. After graduating from secondary school, most of her friends had left for the big cities: Sofia, Plovdiv, or Varna. Two of her classmates had emigrated to find work with their relatives in Spain. There were a handful of girls who stayed behind, but these were mostly the devout Muslim girls. They got married and were rarely seen in public again, and then only if they were wearing their headscarves. Yordanka knew a few of them from school, but they now had children and mostly clustered together at the playgrounds.

"But then you would be here alone," Yordanka told her father. "There would be no one to look after you."

"Well, I have my sister in the village. I could go and live there for a while and let her take care of me. You are too young to have to look after an old man like me."

"But daddy . . ."

"No, I mean it. You did not go to university because of me, and I know you would have been a great student. If you go to Sofia you could find a good job, and then perhaps you could send some money home."

Yordanka stared at him.

"Well, you know, my small pension is really not enough for the two of us. You will have to find work at some point, and we know that there is no work for young women in Madan. You could find something in Sofia for a while. And then maybe sit those entrance exams and go to the university."

So Yordanka had accepted the eighteen leva that it cost her to buy a bus ticket to Sofia from her father. She had a window seat on the bus. As the vehicle wound its way through the precarious Rhodope Mountains, Yordanka daydreamed about finding a good job where she would earn a decent wage. Enough to send at least a hundred leva home to her father and his sister and enough to have a nice room in a shared apartment with other young women her age. And enough to buy herself a new pair of low-rise jeans; the ones that she knew were in fashion in the big cities. Maybe she would meet someone in Sofia, a nice boy with a good job who would take her out to dinner sometimes and pay for her coffee in the morning. All of the boys she had known in Madan were too poor to pay for anything. Although she had lost her virginity in her second year of high school, Yordanka had only had a handful of lovers, and they had all left to go to the cities. Since her mother died she had felt empty. She had no interest in boys, and for their part the boys in Madan showed no interest in her. They all knew that she was looking after her father on her own. That is how it is in a small town. Everybody knows everybody else's business.

As she sat on the bus staring out the window at the lush green hills, she thought of the last boy who made love to her after the disco party at the municipal pool two summers ago. She reached up and grabbed a handful of her curls, remembering how he had whispered into her ear and planted wet kisses on the exact spot where her neck became her shoulder.

"You have such magnificent hair," he told her as his hand had slid up her T-shirt. "Only Greek goddesses have hair like you."

Yordanka had giggled. She knew that she was too short, that she was too chubby, that her breasts were two different sizes and were too small in proportion to the thickness of her waist. But she had great hair. She had rolled her partner over on his back so that she could straddle him, allowing a massive tangle of dark curls to fall over her bare breasts and rounded belly. The boy had literally gasped at the sight of all of that hair tumbling toward his chest.

"Maybe I will fall in love in Sofia," Yordanka thought. "Maybe someone will rescue me."

When she arrived in Sofia, she had the name and address of another girl who had moved to Sofia from Madan. When Yordanka went to the apartment, the girl's roommates, two twenty-one-year-olds from the Christian city of Russe, said that Yordanka's contact had left. They did not know where she was. And they did not want to room with any more "whores from Madan," slamming the door in her face. Yordanka had only thirty leva left and did not know where to go. She had the sense to go to Sofia University, the school she had once dreamed of attending and looked at the notice boards for students searching for roommates. Yordanka knew that all of the students in Sofia lived in a neighborhood called Students' City, and she hoped that there would be someone who would take her in. She pulled a few notices off the board and went to a newspaper kiosk to buy a five leva phone card, the smallest denomination they came in.

She called the first number.

"Hello."

"Hello, I am calling about the room."

"Are you a student?"

"No, but I . . ."

"Where are you from?"

"I just came in from Madan."

The voice on the other end of the phone laughed. "I am sorry, but I don't want to live with a peasant."

The phone clicked off. Yordanka checked her balance. She dialed the second number.

"Hello."

"Yes, I am calling about the room."

"I already rented it. Sorry."

The person hung up.

Yordanka stared at the third notice. "Female student in studio apartment seeks roommate who does not mind sharing close quarters."

Yordanka dialed the number but there was no answer. She left a message. "Hi, my name is Yordanka Todorova, and I am a student," then she paused. "I am a student of German philology at the Sofia University and . . . and . . . well . . . I just broke up with my boyfriend and don't have a place to stay. I don't mind living in close quarters as long as the rent is not too much. I don't have a mobile phone, so I will call back later this evening. My name is Yordanka Todorova."

She called the fourth number, but got an error message saying that the mobile number subscriber was no longer a customer. Yordanka heaved her duffle bag over her shoulder and plopped down in a nearby coffee shop. She was hungry, tired, and frustrated. She splurged thirty stotinki to buy herself an espresso and then went back to the phone booth.

"Daddy?"

"Hi dear! Are you in Sofia now?"

"Yes," Yordanka said.

"How is it going? Do you have a place to sleep tonight?"

"Yes," she lied. "I have found a roommate in Students' City."

"Wonderful! And do you have any leads on a good job?"

"Yes, I think so. I saw an ad for a secretary position in an Italian import-export firm."

"Wonderful. Your mother would be so proud of you. You are so much like her, you know."

"I hope so," Yordanka said under her breath.

"I love you, dear. Please take care of yourself."

"I love you, Daddy. Look for a postal transfer from me in the next month or so."

"You are a good girl, Yordanka."

"Dad, I've got to go."

"Okay dear. Please call me and tell me when you find a job."

Yordanka went back to the student notice board and pulled down a few more notices of students looking to share their lodgings. After three more calls, she got through to a young woman who sounded eager for Yordanka to come and look at the place. Yordanka took a bus out to Students' City and met her future roommate an hour later.

"You won't have your own room," the girl had explained, but I am only asking for forty leva a month. How much is your stipend?"

Yordanka stared down at the thin foam mattress on the floor of a common living area that she was trying to rent. There was a small dresser for her clothes topped with a small shadeless lamp. "Well," she hesitated, deciding to tell the truth. "I am not a student yet. I have to work for a little bit before I can start my studies."

The woman looked at Yordanka and then down at the floor. "I really only wanted a student."

"Yes, I understand," Yordanka interrupted, "but I did not want to lie to you and tell you I was a student. I've just come to Sofia, I don't know anyone here, and I can pay you fifty leva a month if you'll just give me a chance."

"Do you have a job yet?"

It was Yordanka's turn to look down at the ground. "No, not yet."

"Can you pay me the first month's rent in advance?"

"No. I only have about thirty leva to live on until I get paid."

The young woman did not look happy. She scowled at Yordanka. "Where are you from anyway?"

"From Madan," Yordanka mumbled. She was a village girl in the big city for the first time, and she was certain this student was going to kick her out. She reached down for her bag.

"Wow! I'm from Zlatograd," said the woman, smiling for the first time. "I have some cousins in Madan, I think."

Yordanka nodded and shrugged.

The young woman looked her up and down once more. "It is hard coming to Sofia for the first time. Everyone is so mean and mistrustful. I came two years ago, and it was really difficult for me, too. I guess I have become a bit of a *Sofianka* myself."

Yordanka said nothing.

"There are a lot of assholes in Sofia; that is the first thing you should learn. But I think that most people are generally good. We just all get so tired of being lied to and cheated all the time." The woman paused and considered Yordanka's bad, out-of-fashion clothes and communist-era, nylon duffle. "You seem nice enough. I am going to let you stay."

Yordanka's heart leapt.

"You will have to pay me fifty leva a month like you said, and I expect it out of your first salary."

"Yes, of course."

"And you won't be allowed to have any guests. Especially men, is that clear?"

"Of course. Of course."

"And you will have to keep it clean in here. And you can't take long showers."

Yordanka nodded, feeling light.

"Okay," said the young woman, "My name is Nelly. You can stay here tonight, and I will go and get a key made for you. There are a lot of stores in the center that are looking for sales girls. You should try there in the morning."

Sure enough, Yordanka found a job in a shoe store the very next day. She was to work six days a week (not on Mondays) from 10:00 a.m. to 8:00 p.m., and she would be paid 250 leva a month with the possibility of earning 300 if she was reliable and honest. Yordanka had been overjoyed with her luck and had taken Nelly out for a glass of white wine after her first working day. She called her father to tell him that she had a job, and he sent her another thirty leva to help her get through the rest of the month. It was difficult to live on so little money; she ate only plain bread and drank water on most days. She started to lose weight quickly, which made her look prettier than she had ever looked in her life. She could no longer afford to put olive oil in her hair, but she did wash it every day so that it was always clean. The first month was a hard one, but Yordanka had believed that she was going to make it in Sofia after all.

She had already planned everything that she was going to do on the day she was expecting her first salary after working twenty-four days in the shoe store. She would immediately pay Nelly her fifty leva rent and send fifty leva to her father. She would buy a pair of secondhand low-rise jeans now that her old clothes were getting too baggy. She also had her eye on a pair of dangly chandelier earrings in a "one lev" store. And she would buy herself some ground beef and make some meatballs; she had not eaten meat in the last month. Yordanka was craving it desperately.

The manager walked into the store at 2:00 p.m. on payday, looking around. He was a thick-shouldered man in his mid-thirties with a clean-shaven head, but a babyish face. Yordanka could see that there was almost

A shoe store in Sofia.

no stubble on his chin, and thought that he was probably incapable of growing a beard. He seemed amiable enough, although he was always in a hurry. The manager usually only came around at closing time to take the money from the cash register. Yordanka was to keep a careful inventory of how many shoes were sold and for how much in a written accounting book. The manager would check this log against the money in the register to make sure there were no discrepancies.

"You have done well," he said, smiling at her. "It looks good in here, and I hear that you are on time every morning."

Yordanka nodded and smiled.

"Good. The trouble is that we are having some financial difficulties and might have to sell the store. We need to move more merchandise."

"It seems like you have sold a lot of shoes this month."

"No, we haven't. We bought too many sandals, and it will soon be time to sell boots. We'll have to start discounting these summer shoes. I want you to change the prices on all of these sandals in the window. Mark them thirty percent down."

"Of course."

The manager reached into his suit jacket, and gently laid a hundred leva on the counter. "There are your wages for the month."

"But," Yordanka said.

"What?" the manager asked.

"My salary is supposed to be 250 leva a month."

The man stared at her. He sighed, nodding his head and placing a hand on her shoulder in a friendly way. "Well, business is not good this month. We'll give you the rest with your salary next month. Make sure you mark these sandals down before you leave tonight. Okay?"

"Okay," she said.

He strode out of the shop before Yordanka could think of anything else to say.

She stared down at the hundred leva on the counter and tried hard not to be disheartened. They would pay her four hundred leva next month, and she could send one hundred leva to her father then. She set aside her fifty leva for rent and resolved to live another month on bread and water. She just had to rough it for the first few months; she would make it through.

Yordanka busied herself with the shoes in the window, removing all of the price placards and prepared to replace them. She worked behind a little desk, making new placards showing the old price handwritten in black ink crossed out with the new price written below it. A woman paused at the store window for a moment and then walked in through the door.

"How much are those sandals?"

"Which ones?"

"The ones with the rope laces around the ankles."

Out of habit, Yordanka blurted the old price. "Fifty leva."

"Do you have them in a size thirty-six?"

"Let me check." She went back into the storeroom and found the size. "Yes, here they are."

The woman tried them on, walked around the store for a few minutes, glancing at her feet in the low mirrors.

"Good," she said. "These will match perfectly."

She reached into her wallet and dropped a fifty leva bill onto the counter. "Just throw my old ones in a bag for me, won't you?"

Yordanka dutifully scooped up the shoes the woman had worn into the store and put them in the box. The woman grabbed the bag and left the store, calling a breezy "thanks" over her shoulder on her way out. Yordanka looked down at the new price placard she was making. The top number in black was fifty and the bottom number in red was thirty-five. She had not rung the sale into the cash register. The owner would never know that she sold the shoes for fifty leva instead of for thirty-five. And she really needed the money.

But I must not steal, Yordanka thought; then I will be fired for sure. This is not my money. And if the store does better then maybe they will raise my wages to three hundred leva a month.

But the next month the same thing happened again. Yordanka figured out that the woman in the newspaper kiosk across the street was spying on her, making sure she did not open the shop late or take long breaks. But Yordanka was always on time, and since the sandals had been marked down to thirty percent off, they had been flying off of the shelves. On payday, however, the manager once again gave her one hundred leva. He told her that the owners were having some troubles and promised her that he would personally make sure she got paid everything she was owed with her next month's wages. "Once the boots come in we'll finally start making some real money, and we will be able to give you everything you are owed."

His baby face was sweet and he seemed sincere, but Yordanka looked at his clothes and shoes and his watch and knew that he was not living on bread and water like she was. Yordanka was angry, but was not sure who to blame. She had never actually met the owner. She said nothing to the manager, who was studying her face. She berated herself for not taking the extra fifteen leva when she had had the chance.

"And you will have to get some new clothes," the manager said. "You look unprofessional with your clothes hanging off of you like that."

Yordanka swallowed. She was clearly in no position to buy any new clothes since he had not paid her the full amount of her salary for two months. She said nothing. The manager carefully counted the money in the till.

"I know it's hard right now, but you will get it all next month," he said, "But if I ever find that the till is short, you will be fired immediately, and you won't get anything. And I will make sure that you never get another job in Sofia again. Do you understand?"

She nodded.

Another month went by. Yordanka was desperate. She had sent no money home to her father, and the lack of food was finally causing her hair to fall out. She took a shower one morning toward the end of the third month and great handfuls of hair tangled themselves around her fingers. That morning, Yordanka took an extra five minutes gathering up all of the stray hair on the bathroom floor, sobbing and missing her father and her home in Madan. She had not met any men, she barely ever saw Nelly (who was now too busy with her studies), and she was ravenous for food. Yordanka had spent all her time in a store selling women's shoes and had no money to go out. She sometimes lingered in the doorway and watched people walking past, but mostly she sat behind her little desk and listened to the radio. If they did not pay her this month, she would have to go home.

That night Yordanka told Nelly about her problems with the shoe store, and Nelly encouraged her to find another job. Yordanka was still hopeful that the manager would live up to his promises and pay her the wages she was due. Nelly was not so optimistic.

"Yordanka, he is cheating you. He now owes you 550 leva. He will fire you before he pays you."

"He couldn't do that!"

"Of course he could. And there won't be anything you can do about it."

"I could go to the police."

"Ha! In Sofia? The police will do nothing. Not unless you are prepared to bribe them. And you have no money."

"But I've been a perfect employee."

"And there are a hundred girls like you who will take your job in a minute."

"So what am I supposed to do?"

"If he only checks the till at night, then just take out the money he owes you on your pay day and leave. Find another job."

"But that is stealing!"

"No, those are your wages!"

"I could not do that."

"Well, you better take at least fifty so you can pay me the rent that you owe me before you are back on the bus to Madan!"

Nelly was right. Yordanka went to work on the day she was to be paid and the manager stormed in at about 2:00 p.m.

"You've been late every day this week!" he said, his baby face contorted with anger.

This was a lie.

Yordanka inhaled sharply. "That is not true. I have been here every day on time. Like I always am."

"I have people watching you, and you have been late. You are getting lazy. I bet you have a new boyfriend, right?" He was shouting at her.

"I've been here almost every day for ten hours for three months."

"Get out!"

"What?"

"You are fired," the manager said.

"Why?"

"Because you are lazy and you look like a slob. No one wants to buy shoes from you. Look at yourself, with your baggy clothes and your overgrown hair."

Yordanka's mouth fell open. "But . . . but . . . you owe me 550 leva. Those are my wages."

"I don't owe you anything." He reached into the till and threw fifty leva at her. "That's all you deserve. Now get out of my store. And don't come back here again, or I'll have you arrested for stealing."

Yordanka's mouth fell open.

"Get out now!" the manager commanded.

Yordanka snatched her purse and the fifty leva and ran out of the store, huge tears of anger and frustration spilling down her cheeks. She started walking back toward the bus stop to Students' City but stopped. She only had fifty leva and that was what she owed Nelly for the last month's rent. She would have nothing left. If she wanted to take the bus home to Madan she would have to call her father and ask him to send a postal transfer.

Yordanka went straight to the central bus station, not even bothering to pick up her few possessions from Nelly's flat. She was sorry to run out like that, but what else was she supposed to do? She wished she had never come to Sofia. It was a humiliating defeat.

As the bus maneuvered its way through the traffic out of the city, Yordanka stared at the prostitutes waving at the cars and trucks from the side of the road. They were young girls like her. Maybe they had worked as shop girls first, too. She was glad she was getting out of the big city and going home to her father. She guessed that those girls had nowhere to go home to.

The memories of Sofia rushed through her mind as she walked back toward her father's apartment with his medicine. She would have to try to get another job in Smolyan. Even if she had to commute, at least she did not have to pay rent to sleep on a mattress on the floor.

She took the minibus to Smolyan the next day and walked around the city inquiring for work. There was nothing, not even a café looking for a waitress. If she studied for an entrance exam she might be able to get a spot in a university and earn a stipend. That would take a year. How would she help her father in the meantime? She had already signed up for social support from the municipality, but this was only sixty leva a month and would expire after half a year.

The late autumn air was cool. It would be winter soon. Her father had not done so well the past two winters. Yordanka worried about his health. If he died, she would be alone. The thought frightened her. She walked a little farther out of the old center of the city in hopes that she might find some café or store in need of help. In the outer neighborhoods most of the businesses were family owned. Her chances were next to nothing.

It was in one of the neighborhoods above the city library when she saw the sign a second time.

"We buy hair. Up to 100 leva for long, healthy hair."

A hundred leva was a lot of money in Madan. It would get them through the next month until Yordanka could find a job. She reached back and grabbed a handful of hair, lifting it off of her neck and shaking it out.

Never, she thought.

"Well, it is not like it won't grow back," replied a small voice of doubt in her head.

"No way," Yordanka bit her lip, pushing this other voice out of her mind.

"A hundred leva is more than three months of your father's medicine," the voice cajoled. "And it is only hair."

Yordanka spent another hour wandering through Smolyan, looking into shop windows for "help wanted" signs. She was hungry. She was getting cold. At about 3:30 p.m. she was becoming light-headed when her eyes settled on a sign in the lower corner of the window of a hair salon. The same sign: "We buy hair. Up to 100 leva for long, healthy hair."

She walked into the salon. "I would like to sell my hair."

A woman eyed her greedily and smiled. "Oh, you have such lovely hair! Are you sure?"

"Yes," Yordanka said. She sat down in one of the nearest chairs and closed her eyes. If she did not do it right away, she knew she would lose her nerve. She loved her hair. She could not even imagine what she would look like without it. "Just do it. I need the money. My father is ill . . ."

She did not finish her sentence. The woman was weighing her hair with her hands and looking at the ends.

"These are natural curls, yes?"

"Yes. It is long and healthy."

"Oh, yes. Beautiful hair."

"I will get a hundred leva?"

"You should get more," the hairdresser said, "but that is what we can afford to give you for it."

"Do it then," Yordanka said, gazing at herself one last time in the mirror.

It was gone in less than five minutes—tied up into a ponytail and cut off.

"Would you like me to style your hair now?" asked the hairdresser.

"Yes, please," said Yordanka, already regretting her decision. How long would it take to grow back? What would her father say? It was the right thing to do, she told herself. She had no choice until she found a job.

"Oh dear," the hairdresser said.

"What?"

"Have you dyed your hair?"

"No, never," replied Yordanka.

"Oh, yes, you have," said the hairdresser. "It is very obvious once it is cut. The inner shaft is a different color."

Yordanka's eyes widened. "I have never, never dyed my hair! My hair is naturally brown and naturally curly."

"I can't sell dyed hair for as much as I can sell natural hair, my dear."

"What are you saying?"

"I am afraid I can only give you sixty leva for this dyed hair."

"My hair is not dyed. You are a liar! You are trying to cheat me!"

The woman looked hurt. She lowered her voice and spoke in a sweet and innocent tone. "Oh, no, I would never do that. Look, see for yourself, the inner shaft is a different color."

"But I have never dyed my hair."

"Well, why don't you just take it and try to sell it to someone else. You'll see that they will tell you the same thing. Anyone who deals with hair can tell you the difference between dyed and natural color."

The hairdresser offered up the severed ponytail of Yordanka's long brown curls. "Go ahead and take it. Sell it yourself."

Yordanka felt all of the blood rushing to her face. She grabbed the ponytail and caressed it in her hands. If she could have stitched each strand back onto her head she would have. But what was she going to do with her hair now that it was already cut off?

"You told me you would pay me one hundred leva."

"That is because your hair color looked quite natural."

"That is because it is natural!"

"If you say so. Go ahead and take it. Sell it somewhere else. I am telling you that you won't get more than sixty leva. And you will have to go all the way to Plovdiv to sell it, because I am the only buyer in Smolyan."

"I am going to go to the police!"

"Go ahead," the woman said, smiling. "And say hello to my cousin while you are there. He's the police chief. I'm sure he'll be willing to help you."

Yordanka felt the tears burning her eyes. The taste of bile filled her mouth as her stomach clenched and unclenched in contortions of rage and despair. She wanted to attack this woman, this deceptive bitch. To scratch at her eyes with her fingernails. To bite her. She glanced over at the haircutting scissors on the counter and imagined plunging them into the woman's neck or cutting out her tongue or at the very least cutting off what remained of her already rather short hair.

But Yordanka's hair was already gone. "Just give me my sixty leva, you liar." Yordanka spat.

"Fifty leva, my dear," the woman said sweetly, opening a drawer and pulling out a fifty leva note. "I charge ten leva for the haircut. It says so right on the door."

Yordanka grabbed the banknote, threw her hair on the floor and ran out into the cold late November air. She kept running until she reached a small masonry bridge at the outskirts of town, near the main road that led to Plovdiv. She stood there for a long while, staring down at the water below and thinking that she would like to throw herself in. But the bridge was not really very high.

The night fell slowly and the air got colder. She would have to make her way back to the bus station if she was going to catch the last minibus to Madan. She gazed out over the river and saw two women standing on the other side of the road to Plovdiv. They were waving at the cars driving by, cajoling them to stop. If she didn't know better, she would have thought they were two hitchhikers. They were prostitutes. Just like the ones she had seen leaving Sofia.

Without thinking too much, Yordanka walked down toward the road to get a closer look at them. One was tall and slim, her long legs encased in sheer black hose and teetering on four- or five-inch stilettos. She wore a simple black minidress with black see-through netting that started beneath her small breasts and stretched down to five or six centimeters below her navel, exposing a wide swath of midriff through the thin fabric. She had long, straight, dark hair and wore bright red lipstick that stood out even from across the road. The second woman was shorter and more round. She wore a white top, and Yordanka could clearly see the outline of her bra. There were slight bulges above and below where the bra cut into the skin under the woman's arms. She had long, bleached blond hair with four centimeters of black roots at the crown of her head. She was heavily made up and wore the same bright red lipstick as the first woman. As each car or truck passed, they leaned over and waved furiously for the drivers to stop.

Yordanka approached them. They glanced over at her but did not stop their waving.

"How much do you charge?"

The bottle blond looked at her. "Why do you want to know?"

"I'm just . . . curious."

The blond woman eyed her closely and stopped her waving. The brunette continued trying to lure the drivers that ignored them. There were prostitutes on all of the major roads in Bulgaria.

"Well, you see the price varies depending on the car," she said, with an almost motherly tone in her voice. She had guessed Yordanka's intentions. "Most drivers only want a blowjob, so that runs between twenty and fifty leva. Twenty leva for the Bulgarian truckers, and thirty leva for the foreign truckers; they are workingmen after all. We charge forty for all private cars, and sometimes fifty if it is a nice car with Sofia or Varna plates or if it is a foreign car."

Yordanka listened without interrupting.

"As for sex, well blowjobs are more work for us than sex. And it's mostly the truckers who want sex and for you to spend the night with them in the cab. They get lonely, you see. For sex, we charge a flat rate of thirty leva for the Bulgarians and forty leva for the foreigners. If they want you for the whole night it is fifty either way, with the option of a blowjob in the morning for an additional twenty leva. We sort of give a discount to the truckers, you see."

"And do they always pay you?"

"Well, in our business, my dear, you always ask for the money in advance. And yes, they almost always pay. They are usually pretty happy with our services."

Yordanka hesitated and looked around to make sure no one was watching her. Her father would die if word got back that she was seen in Smolyan conversing with a couple of prostitutes. "Do you get a lot of customers?"

The blonde shrugged. "Look, my dear, this is not a good way to make a living if you can avoid it. You are young. Go to school. Go to Sofia and find a proper job."

"I've tried that," Yordanka murmured under her breath.

"Well, if you are seriously thinking about this you have to be prepared to lie a lot. Your family will never accept you if they find out. And there is no going back. It is hard to get out once you start. A lot of girls think they can do it just for a little while, but it doesn't work that way. So think really hard, girl, before you make a decision like this one. It will change the rest of your life."

It was a thoughtful conversation with someone that Yordanka would not have spoken to under other circumstances. She mumbled a thank you and turned to walk toward the bus station before she missed the last bus back to Madan.

"One more thing," the blond woman with the too-tight bra called after Yordanka. "If you are thinking about it, it would be best to grow out your hair. You look like a boy. Men like long hair, you know. Long, feminine hair."

CHAPTER 5 SHOPAHOLIC IN EASTERN EUROPE, 1998–2006

In the late 1990s one of the most difficult things about doing research in Eastern Europe was the dearth of retail opportunities. As an American who tended to shop her way out of most life dramas, the paucity of consumption possibilities in Bulgaria taught me how much Westerners like me took for granted our consumer culture. Over the years, however, I have watched Bulgaria evolve from a veritable retail wasteland, where procuring essential goods and services was a feat requiring all of the perseverance and tracking skills of a Louisiana bloodhound, into a country brimming with luxurious retail oases where opulent, new shopping malls spring forth from the earth like magic beanstalks and where compact islands of consumerism are surrounded by oceans of abject poverty.

In 1997 when I first started researching Bulgaria, the country had just experienced a total economic meltdown. Hyperinflation had caused prices to rise exponentially. For instance, a tube of toothpaste that cost four leva one week would cost four hundred leva just weeks later. As a result, those who had been frugal and saved money saw the value of their savings disappear. On the other hand, those who had been in debt rejoiced as the sums they owed became insignificant. Wages were not indexed to inflation, and unscrupulous traders hoarded scarce goods and then price gouged the population. The economy imploded.

The economic chaos precipitated a sudden change of government, as disenchanted voters demanded immediate new elections. During my first few months of official fieldwork in June, July, and August 1998, the new government had instituted a currency board with the Bulgarian lev pegged to the German mark. Things were returning to "normal." I lived with Hristo in his parents' apartment and had no need of procuring any essential household items. I was happy to subsist on the fresh fruits and vegetables that are so abundant in the summer months in a largely agricultural country. It was only when I returned for fourteen months in 1999–2000 and had to set up my own household that I began to understand the difficulties one faced in the acquisition of almost anything beyond the bare Bulgarian basics of bread, beer, and white and yellow cheese.

It did not matter if you had the money to spend; there was very little to buy. The choice of most goods was miserably limited, and the prices were either ridiculously expensive or embarrassingly cheap as mobsters and the nouveau riche glutted themselves on Western European designer imports while the rest of Bulgarians made do with whatever random goods were shuttle traded or smuggled into the country from Turkey and sold in large outdoor markets. The concept of one-stop shopping was nonexistent. Stores were segregated by the type of goods they sold; only in the smaller villages were there single shops that sold bread, *rakiya* (Bulgarian brandy), nails, and fertilizers over the same counter. In most "food stock" stores you were not allowed to examine any of the goods before purchasing them. Instead, you waited behind a counter and pointed at the things you thought you wanted while the grouchiest grandmother in the country reluctantly took them down from the shelves and decided (using some unknown criteria) whether you were worthy enough to have these crackers sold to you. Even TZUM, the Central Department Store in the capital city Sofia, was full of random booths selling a sparse selection of inferior goods. The strangest thing about all of this, however, was that most people I spoke to seemed to think that the shopping scene was pretty good, at least compared to what it had been before.

Although I never lived in Bulgaria during the communist period, there were still some shopkeepers who had not quite adjusted their practices in line with the new market economy. Once when I was returning to the United States for a visit, I decided to bring my friends and family some boxes of a particular kind of Bulgarian herbal tea that I liked. There was a

A small shop in the countryside.

small store in my neighborhood that sold it, so I did not think to get it in the center of town. It was the evening before my plane was scheduled to leave, and I was almost finished packing. I walked down to the shop and saw that they had eight boxes of the tea on the shelf behind the shopkeeper.

"Eight boxes of tourist tea, please," I said in Bulgarian.

"Eight?" The woman said. She was an older woman in her late fifties or sixties who chewed on her inner cheeks when she was not speaking. She wore a plain, shapeless blue dress, and her hair was dyed a purplish black. "That is my entire stock. You can have two."

I did not understand her and thought that maybe she did not understand me. "Please, I would like to buy eight boxes of tourist tea."

"No. I said you could have two."

I thought maybe she thought that I was asking to buy them on credit. I took out a twenty leva bill. "But I can buy all of them. I have enough money."

"No," she repeated. "I won't have enough for other people if I sell them all to you."

"But you can order more!"

"But that will take some time. I will not have an empty shelf in my store."

"But isn't your goal to sell them all anyway?"

"What do you need eight boxes of tea for? Two is enough for you."

"I am buying them for presents," I said. It occurred to me that she might want to charge me more money, but I think she just really didn't want me to buy all eight boxes. It did not seem right to her. "Can you at least sell me four?"

She thought about this for a moment and looked at the twenty leva note in my hand.

"If you sell me four then you will have the money now. You can order more before the other four get sold."

"Three," she said. "No one needs more than three boxes of tea."

I paid for the three boxes and later sent my husband, Hristo, down to buy three more. When he returned with only two, I did not even ask what had happened. He murmured something about the shopkeeper being a "red grandmother" and told me that I had no idea what it had been like before. You could not just go into a shop and get whatever you liked.

It was after this incident that I became more curious to understand how shopping had worked before 1989. Central planning was supposed to alleviate what communists believed to be the exploitative fluctuations of prices that resulted from the natural rhythms of supply and demand. Monopolistic price gouging was considered an immoral result of capitalist free markets, so the state controlled the production and distribution of all goods and services in the economy. The government allocated its scarce resources toward health care, education, electricity, water, heat, and housing at the expense of consumer goods like clothing and cosmetics. Having the government decide what products to make guaranteed that people would have their basic needs met before they "wasted" their money on what were considered inessential luxury items.

Here it might be helpful to digress and give a hypothetical example of how central planning worked in practice. Let's say that the government decided that Bulgaria should produce a new perfume; a planning committee of economists and enterprise and cooperative directors (usually men) would be convened. The first decision might be what kind of perfume to make. Bulgaria has been exporting rose oil since the seventeenth century, and under communism rose oil exports to Western perfumeries were one of Bulgaria's key exports to the capitalist world. Many of the most expensive perfumes in the world were (and are) based on Bulgarian rose oil. The central planners did their best to take aesthetic considerations into account given their supply constraints. It would therefore be decided that one perfume based on rose oil would be produced for the domestic market.

This perfume based on rose oil would need packaging. The planners knew that Western perfumes had elaborate glass bottles with unique and artistic designs, and that this was part of their appeal. But the planning committee would have limited resources and might argue that the packaging was irrelevant to the purpose of perfume—to make someone smell nice—and would decide to use basic glass bottles in order to cut costs. Western perfumes also had atomizers, but there was no domestic facility to produce atomizers nor were there any available from brother socialist countries within the Council for Mutual Economic Assistance (CMEA), the Communist trading bloc. Our planning committee would know that it would be foolish to ask for the hard currency necessary to import atomizers from the West. Trade between communist countries was conducted in a barter-like fashion, but Bulgaria needed hard currency (that is, Western currencies) to buy goods outside of the CMEA. This hard currency was jealously guarded by the state in order to import key industrial goods to support Bulgaria's factories, and the Bulgarian Foreign Trade Bank was unlikely to give a hard currency loan for consumer items. Bulgarian perfume would be applied with the finger. Guessing that Bulgarian women might be unhappy with the packaging, the planning committee would instruct the editors of the official state women's magazine, *Zhenata Dnes*, to run an article discussing the value of the actual perfume versus the packaging of major Western brands in order to educate women on the irrationality of paying for pretty glass.

Once the scent and the packaging were decided upon, then would come the difficult process of figuring out how many units of perfume to produce. Complicated statistical models would be employed to project the expected demand for rose oil perfume among Bulgarian women. First they might start with the total population of Bulgarian women and assume that half of the women still had bottles of perfume left over from the previous year's quota. Then they might subtract a percentage that represents all women over the age of sixty-five by arguing that older women do not wear perfume. Since primary and secondary schools prohibited students from wearing perfume or cosmetics, all girls under the age of eighteen could also be excluded. The planning committee would also take into account the perfumes already available from Poland, Russia, or other socialist brother countries and adjust their number further downward. In the end, the planning committee would propose to produce fifty-seven thousand bottles of rose oil perfume for the given year. Or if it was responsible for a multiyear plan, it would project these numbers out for the next five years given such factors as population growth, graduation rates, future barter agreements, and so forth. This was a difficult task without computers, but the planners did their best to accurately produce a supply of goods that would meet the expected domestic demand.

Once the number of fifty-seven thousand was derived, the planning committee would have the difficult job of coordinating with the rose-growing cooperatives, the rose oil distillers, and the glass manufacturers to ensure that all of the necessary inputs could be had. The rose oil distiller would claim that it did not produce enough attar to meet its predetermined export obligations to the West and to produce fifty-seven thousand bottles of perfume. The maximum they could supply would be for forty thousand bottles. The glass manufacturers would have many other obligations to the heavy industrial enterprises and could only spare enough time on its machines to make thirty-five thousand bottles, and these bottles would have to be half the size of the original plan in order to avoid a timely recalibration of the machinery. The planning committee would try to negotiate these figures upward, but they would eventually have to settle for well below their carefully derived estimate. The final figure would be sent to the appropriate authorities for approval.

In the end, a boom in the Western economies would increase the price and demand for Bulgarian rose oil. The government would decide at the last minute to sell all of that year's rose oil to private French companies for hard currency, arguing that they could then use the francs earned to import perfumes from the West. But then the hard currency earned from the sale of the rose oil is put toward the construction of a new petrochemical factory because Communists prized heavy industry over all other sectors of the economy. Only a small portion of the money is set aside for perfume imports.

So instead of the original fifty-seven thousand bottles the planning committee had intended to produce, they get approval to import ten thousand bottles of French perfume, a number far below its already conservative calculation of domestic demand. Knowing full well that there will be a scarcity of perfume in Bulgaria, the planning committee members are forced to accept that perfume is not really a "need" at all. Each of the planning committee members takes at least ten bottles for his family and friends. The editors of *Zhenata Dnes* run an article on how perfume has gone out of fashion in Paris this year and how French women are preferring to go au natural. Only Bulgarian women with connections would be able to procure a bottle of this French perfume. Other women might be able to buy one from a hard currency store where Western goods were sold for dollars, pounds, and francs. But most women would end up with nothing. The state was able to provide things like housing, education, health care, public transportation, and generous supports for working mothers, but it often failed miserably when it came to providing things like perfume.

As a graduate student in the late 1990s, I understood the idea behind central planning in theory, but it was only after my own hopeless search for a bottle of Calvin Klein's Eternity eau de toilette that I began to understand what it had been like for ordinary people during the command economic period. During the fruitless search for my favorite scent, I had many conversations with women selling cosmetics all around the capital city of Sofia. I soon came to realize that it was absurd for me to be picky about which type of perfume I bought in Bulgaria. I was lucky to have any choice at all. A nice middle-aged woman with orange hair in TZUM eventually convinced me to buy her only bottle of Anais Anais by Cacharel instead, a perfume that I did not even like very much. I learned that most Bulgarians still ordered goods such as perfume from friends and relatives who traveled abroad. If I wanted a bottle of Eternity, I would have to have someone bring it from home.

Part of the problem was that Bulgaria was slow to develop and move beyond its central planning past compared to its socialist brother countries to the northwest. In 1999 when Metro, the first German cash-and-carry opened in Sofia, it was like a small consumer revolution even though there was a whole panoply of rules that had to be followed in order to shop there: you had to be a member (which seemed to require blood samples and the proof of a recent liver biopsy from your maternal grandmother); you had to spend a minimum amount of money on each visit; you were not allowed to shop with children under the age of seven; and so on. Slowly, other foreign stores entered the market and miraculously you could then buy fresh fruits and vegetables in the winter months and there were more than two types of cheese available in the store.

If you had the money.

The new plethora of retail opportunities in Bulgaria threw into sharp relief the economic disparities arising in the country. In particular, there emerged a vast rural and urban divide. Western perfumes and shampoos appeared in the country at the exact moment when the state was no longer able to pay for housing, education, health care, or social supports for new mothers. It is a sad irony that at the exact moment when Bulgaria actually began to have a functioning market economy, there were many families who were forced to remove themselves from the market altogether—returning to subsistence agriculture as a strategy to survive the desperate consequences of high rural un- and underemployment. The growing choice of new goods was always contrasted to the shrinking number of people in the country that could afford to buy them. Furthermore, consumerism had become acutely gendered, and society's ideals of successful masculinity and femininity were increasingly being defined by ownership of the right material accoutrements for your given sex (cars, watches, laptops, and cell phones for men; clothes, purses, jewelry, high-end cosmetics, and silicone implants for women). Most Bulgarians experienced extreme inequality for the first time.

Fast forward now to 2005–2006 when I moved back to the country for eight more months. The capital had become a consumer wonderland. In the spring of 2006 two huge new shopping malls opened in the capital: the Mall of Sofia and Sofia City Center. In addition, TZUM had been completely remodeled, and they were all full of relatively expensive Western brands such as Stephanel, Triumph, Palmers, Nike, and Sisley. In these stores one bra cost the equivalent of a month's salary for most Bulgarians. Many visitors were empty-pocketed window-shoppers who strolled around inside for the air-conditioning during the oppressive Sofia summer heat. In early August 2006 as I meandered through the Mall of Sofia, I could hardly believe that this was the same country where I had resided in the late 1990s. There were shoes and clothes and cell phones and MP3 players and TVs and stereos and household appliances and imported foods and the latest Hollywood movies and even an IMAX theatre showing a 3-D dinosaur film. Curious about the new retail possibilities, I wandered into a cosmetics shop.

A new mall in Sofia, opened in 2005.

Having just spent the last few months living in a tiny town in one of the most rural parts of the Rhodopi Mountains where many families of six or seven somehow manage to survive on 60 leva a month, I was initially shocked by the prices of the seemingly endless variety of Western facial creams, nail polishes, lipsticks, blushes, eyeliners, mascaras, and perfumes even though I desperately wanted to buy something. I could live down in the city of Madan for a month for the price of one Clarins self-tanning sunscreen. I felt a sudden rush of revulsion as I watched two young Bulgarian girls obviously from the upper-middle class spend close to 300 leva on cosmetics when the average monthly per capita salary in the country was still about 155 leva. I turned to leave, feeling the leftist righteousness of a Berkeley graduate swell up in my chest as I abandoned the temptation to purchase something new and expensive just because I had the money and had been deprived of real shopping opportunities for the last ninety days.

And then I saw it.

There on the shelf across from me, like a monument to a past wish that had long remained unfulfilled, sat a hundred milliliter bottle of Eternity Summer. Long after I had abandoned the original scent as too heavy and far too 1990s, good old Calvin had redesigned the fragrance as something lighter and more airy, something more appropriate for the mid-2000s and for my new, more serious identity as an academic and a mom. After one generous test spray against the inside of my wrist, I grabbed a box and went straight to the counter to pay. After all these years, I finally had my Eternity perfume in Bulgaria—as if somehow the history of the country had conspired to meet my basest consumer desires. I left the store feeling that familiar rush of instant gratification, but there was still a voice inside me that wondered if Bulgaria and Bulgarians were really that much better off because the five percent of the population that could afford to shop in that store and acquisitive American researchers like me could now purchase expensive Western perfumes in Sofia.

As I walked out into the bright and burning sunshine, I thought I heard the whispered curses of Communist central planners condemning me to a capitalist purgatory where I would swim in a stew of my own terrible hypocrisy of privilege. And although I had the smug assurance that they were equally as guilty as I, something about that bottle of Eternity perfume has never quite smelled right.

CHAPTER 6   NEW CARPETS FOR OLD KILIMS, 1999

In 1999 in the villages and small towns across Bulgaria there were photocopied white flyers that stated: "New Carpets for Old Kilims." A kilim is a handmade tapestry, woven rug, or carpet, and they can be found throughout the Muslim world from Pakistan to the Balkans. They are simple rugs and traditionally less valuable than the pile rugs for which countries like Turkey or Iran are so famous. Because kilims never developed an export market, their manufacture and design is now considered to be more authentic than pile carpets, which were often produced to satisfy foreign tastes. Kilims are still common in many households and have been a staple domestic handicraft for centuries. They are also remarkably durable. In Bulgaria kilims were usually passed down from parents to their children, and in the 1990s many of the kilims still owned by the peasants in the countryside were made during the Ottoman era over a hundred years earlier. As a result, antique kilims, such as those to be found in households across Bulgaria, are considered quite valuable for serious collectors and have begun to command a higher price on international markets.

I was a Fulbright Fellow in 1999 and had befriended a young Bulgarian art history student who was eager to fashion himself as an expert on Balkan and Turkish antiques. Over the year that I spent living in Bulgaria, Dimitar and I met for drinks on a few occasions with other American graduate students. He was keen to spend a year in the United States doing an internship at Sotheby's or Christie's in New York City and probably hoped that having American friends would increase his chances. He was also one of those Bulgarians who always disappeared to the men's room when the bill came and hoped that someone else would pick up the tab. The truth was that our student stipends were far larger than his and that drinks in Bulgaria were ridiculously cheap for the Americans who had dollars, so it was no big deal. And Dimitar was always willing to help us navigate the university bureaucracy if we had problems.

One evening, after I had just returned to Sofia from some of the Rhodopi Mountain villages where I noticed the flyers I asked Dimitar if he knew anything about them, and he explained the "brilliant" idea behind the carpets for kilims scheme over beers in a cozy, little Irish pub in the center of town. Our conversation highlighted some of the fundamental tensions of moving from a state-run to a free-market economy and how ordinary people became the unwitting victims of a new generation of Bulgarian entrepreneurs able to pursue profit in a society where personal wealth accumulation through trade had once been criminalized.

"It works like this," Dimitar said. "There is some American antique dealer in Sofia who is paying good money for these old kilims. He can authenticate them, so he can't be fooled. He buys them in Bulgaria for a small percentage of the price that he could sell them for in the States. It is good money by Bulgarian standards. So some Bulgarians in Sofia realized that they can probably turn a good profit if they could find a way to get their hands on a bunch of antique kilims."

Dimitar was a rather handsome young man with a fair complexion and coal dark eyes. His hair was black, curly, and cropped close to his scalp, giving him the appearance of being much older than his mere twenty-five years. I was four years older than him, but he seemed far more grown up than me. He dressed impeccably. On the night we met, he wore pressed blue jeans and a crisp white shirt with stainless steel cufflinks in the shape of two squares. He wore a thick stainless steel bracelet on his left wrist. On his right wrist, he wore a very good replica of an Omega watch that he told me he had bought in Istanbul. He looked like the kind of person that one might want to buy an antique kilim from, or at least the type of person whom you would trust to give an accurate valuation of its worth.

"So they went around buying the kilims from peasants?" I asked.

"Oh no, they were far more clever than that. If it was going to be about money, the peasants might not have sold their family heirlooms. They did not know what they were worth, but they did have sentimental value. No, these Bulgarians rented a big truck and filled it with the gaudiest, kitschiest Chinese-manufactured nylon carpets on the market, very colorful, costing at most a couple hundred dollars apiece. Usually they were worth only a hundred dollars. So they show up in these villages and offer a trade. New carpets for old kilims. The villagers would then dig out their old dusty kilims and bring them hoping to get a new carpet, something modern. It's brilliant."

"It's awful," I said.

Dimitar paused and considered me. Dimitar and I had very different views about the introduction of free markets into Bulgaria. I was of the opinion that they had dismantled the state too fast, and Dimitar believed that they had not done it fast enough. For Dimitar, being an entrepreneur and finding new ways to make money was always a good thing; he epitomized the American Horatio Alger spirit and believed that people should be able to pull themselves up by the bootstraps with the right combination of cleverness, dedication, hard work, and a little bit of luck. I, on the other hand, felt that unbridled free markets, especially the kind that were being introduced to Bulgaria in the 1990s, rewarded the worst kind of violent, greedy, and outright criminal behavior, favoring the biggest thugs in society at the expense of the average people. Dimitar felt this was just a "capitalist growing pain" and that all early capitalist economies needed their robber barons. I always argued that if the foundation of a new capitalist society was based on such widespread crime and corruption, it would never be sustainable. You needed the state to regulate.

"Why do you think that it is awful?" he asked.

"Because they are taking the kilims from the peasants for almost nothing and making a killing when they resell them," I said.

"But the peasants wanted the new carpets. And they would not have been able to afford them otherwise. You could say that they were being done a great service."

I eyed him suspiciously.

"It is not like smuggling icons out of the country or famous pieces of art. They are just old carpets that nobody in Bulgaria wants anyway," Dimitar continued.

I thought about this for a moment. It was true that there had been a lot of illegal smuggling of priceless art and antiquities out of the country after the collapse of communism in 1989. In particular, Orthodox icons and old Ottoman, Byzantine, and Thracian coins had been targeted by collectors who saw the chaos that followed the transition as the perfect time to pick up some valuable antiques at a bargain. The lands that comprise modern Bulgaria were the home to several ancient civilizations, and there were also many unexcavated archeological sites that could be looted now that the secret police were no longer watching. Poor and uneducated Bulgarians were more than happy to do the dirty work for a small fee.

"But they are old carpets that are worth a lot of money," I said. "It seems to me that you have a situation where Bulgarians are cheating Bulgarians for the sake of rich, Western middlemen who reap the profit."

"But who else should reap the profit? The state? Is that what you're saying?"

"I did not say that. What does the state have to do with anything?"

Dimitar and I had a tendency to find ourselves in heated debates about a lot of different things, and I could feel one coming on. He was interested in art history, archeology, and the artifacts of the distant past, the world of yesterday's rich people. I was more interested in ethnography and the way ordinary people experienced the recent past and present. We were bound not to see eye to eye on some things, but bringing the state (and by this he meant the Bulgarian Communist state) into the conversation seemed like a particularly egregious non sequitur.

"It has a lot to do with everything," he said, draining the last of his Murphy's Irish Red Ale and waving at the waiter. "Do you want another one?"

"Sure," I said, noticing that my glass was also almost empty and wondering if he was actually offering to buy me a beer with his own money. I picked tentatively at the bowl of french fries between us and said, "It still sounds like a scam to me."

"Look, Kristen," he said, "the peasants want new carpets. They like the new carpets. They are modern and much cleaner than the old, musty kilims that have been sitting around in their houses for ages. They do not have the money to buy the carpets, and it is very unlikely that they will have the money to buy them in the future. They cannot trade vegetables for carpets."

This was very true. During the 1990s the economic situation in Bulgaria had been so bad that many rural Bulgarians had retreated from the market altogether resorting to barter transactions and in-kind trades that circumvented the cash economy. The poverty rate had increased dramatically. People no longer had access to things they could not produce themselves, including electricity and medicine. If there was ever spare money in a household budget, it was quite unlikely that it would be spent on new carpets.

Dimitar continued, "The kilims have no value in Bulgaria. They cannot be sold to anyone but the handful of Western dealers in Sofia. Most peasants don't have cars to drive to Sofia, and it would cost a lot of money for them to take the bus. On the other side, it is only real connoisseurs in the West that want to buy them. The only reason they have value is because there are some people that are willing to pay for them. So the middlemen provide a valuable service. They buy new carpets and transport them to the villages in exchange for old kilims that many families are happy to be rid of anyway. Then they drive the kilims to Sofia and sell them to someone who will make sure they get to the people in the West who want them. There is absolutely nothing wrong with that."

"The new carpets won't last as long as their old kilims, and even if they did, it is still not a good trade. The peasants are only getting a fraction of their kilims' value," I said.

"But without the middlemen, they would not get anything."

"So that makes it okay to cheat people? That is what they are doing, aren't they?" I asked, imaging some poor grandma trading an antique kilim that will be worth thousands of dollars for a cheap plastic rug from China.

Dimitar thought about this for a moment. He twirled the stainless steel bracelet around his wrist as he contemplated what to say. "So, what is the ideal situation in this case? You could have the state intervene and buy up the kilims for a decent price and have them find buyers on the international market."

"Right," I said, "and the difference between the buying and selling price could go to the state budget and be invested in education and health care for the same peasants who gave up their kilims."

"But that is just socialism all over again . . ."

"So?"

"So what if the people don't want education? What if they just want new carpets? Who is the state to tell them how to spend their money?" Dimitar

Todor Zhikov, Bulgaria's official head of state for thirty-five years. Theoretically, this one man had decision-making power over the country's entire economy.

asked. "And who is going to guarantee that the elites in the state won't pocket the money and give themselves privileges that no one else has?"

"But," I said, now finishing the last swallows of my beer, "why is that any worse than some Brit or American making a huge profit off of the poor people in a country? At least if the state is the middleman then the wealth stays in the country."

"Not if the elites dump it in a Swiss bank for safe keeping until they are out of office."

"There is a chance of that, yes, but at least it is illegal. Corruption of public officials is illegal. They are not allowed to get rich by exploiting their office. But businessmen can? There are no controls on foreigners taking profits out of the country. That is just good business." I shifted uncomfortably in my seat, fearing that our debate was turning into an argument. "It seems to me, at least in a democracy, that it is better to be exploited by a democratically elected government than by a handful of greedy foreign businessmen intent on making a quick profit and moving on to the next vulnerable country."

"Well," Dimitar said as the waiter brought us two more beers, "I think markets are more efficient. There is no way that any government could get into the buying and selling of antiques and be any good at it. Nobody is forcing the peasants to sell their kilims or to trade them in for carpets. It is their own free choice."

"But they don't know the true value of their kilims. I am sure they would not be trading them if they knew how much they were worth."

"No, they probably wouldn't, but they could get that information if they really wanted to."

"How?" I blurted out. "Who are they going to ask?"

"Well, they could write a letter . . ."

"Oh come on, be serious. They are poor people living from day to day, trying to survive. They don't understand the new rules of the game, that it is now okay to buy low and sell high."

Dimitar paused here. He drank his beer, which deposited a small white mustache of foam on his upper lip before he quickly licked it off. "Well, okay. I grant you that there is no perfect information here. And yes, the peasants are not being apprised of the true value of their possessions. But what matters is that without the profit motive, there will be no trade. And without trade there would be no new wealth creation. The carpets for kilims scheme is the perfect example of a case where everyone wins. The peasants get new carpets, the middlemen get a fee, and the rich people in the West have something that they could not otherwise get. That is merely the way the world works, and I think it is a clever way to get the antiques into the hands of the people who care about them the most and who will take care of them the most. Let's not forget that these are part of history. They have to be looked after, not trampled on by goats and chickens."

"They could be put in museums," I ventured.

"And they will be. Some private collectors will inevitably donate them to or lend them to museums."

"Western museums."

"Of course, Western museums. Who in Bulgaria would go to a museum to look at a kilim? By getting them to the West, Bulgarian material culture has the best chances of being preserved for future generations."

"That sounds about as paternalistic as advocating for a state that will give people health care instead of cheap plastic carpets. The key thing is that these people really need the money, a lot more than the middlemen do, and certainly more than rich antique collectors in the West. You know how bad life is in the countryside these days. Bulgarians are living as they did in the nineteenth century, working hard to eke out a living from the land. They are good and honest people, and they are being deceived and cheated no matter what you say."

Dimitar laughed. "They are stupid, greedy peasants who would do the same thing if they had the opportunity. I think it's a brilliant scheme."

I took a large swallow of my beer. "Well, I don't. It's taking advantage of poor people. Playing on their ignorance."

"So you think these beautiful antique kilims should just be left in Bulgaria, to be destroyed or simply thrown away?"

"I think the peasants should be paid what they are worth."

"That will never happen. Not under socialism, not under capitalism, not under any economic system that I am aware of. The world just doesn't work that way."

"Well, it should," I said. "It seems wrong to me that the people who get rich are the ones most willing to lie and steal."

Dimitar shrugged and drank his beer. I munched on a french fry.

"There is always going to be a sucker. There is nothing you can do about that."

"Well," I said, "you can decrease the rewards for being an asshole."

"There are always rewards for being an asshole."

It was a mere reflection on his part, but it came out as a closing statement. Our heated conversation stopped. Dimitar looked down at his fake Omega watch and drank some more beer. I knew there was no more point in arguing.

I watched him carefully, thinking about the mess Bulgaria was in. There were mafia thugs everywhere. The police were corrupt. The courts were useless. There was no reason to believe that anyone would be able to restore order. This *was* the so-called robber baron era of Bulgarian capitalism, where the wealth of the many was concentrated in the hands of a few. Dimitar was just trying to make sure that he didn't get stepped on like the rest of the suckers. In a world full of assholes, Dimitar believed that an individual asshole working for his own self-interest was better than the state-employed asshole supposedly working for the interests of the people. He thought this was a better system. I really wasn't so convinced.

I waved for the waiter to bring us our bill and stood up to go to the ladies room. Dimitar would have to pick up his own tab tonight.

Ani was tall and thin, with straight, golden-brown hair that fell to her shoulders. Her skin was tan, and her eyes were hazel. She would have been a very pretty girl save for the prominent nose that seemed too big for the otherwise delicate features of her face. She also bit her nails incessantly; they were chewed down to the raw flesh of her fingertips. Despite her nervous habit, she was friendly and open, smiling often and compulsively refilling my teacup whenever I emptied it. Her clothes were loose and modest, a wide pair of brown palazzo pants with a white linen, long-sleeve, button-down shirt. At a time of year when most Bulgarian young women Ani's age would be wearing halter tops and mini-skirts, her clothes made her look older and more conservative. At first I assumed that this was her professional look for the office, but she soon informed me that she was a part of the ethnic Turkish minority in Bulgaria, a Muslim minority that was a remnant of the Ottoman imperial presence in the Balkans before Bulgaria's independence in 1878. Ani then quickly assured me that she was allowed to dress however she wanted but that she did not want to make her uncle feel uncomfortable. Ani kept her head uncovered but thought it best not to expose too much skin. Her uncle was responsible for her during the summer.

Ani was about to turn twenty when I met her in 2000. She had just finished her first year of university, and she was working for her uncle as a reservations manager in a hotel in the Bulgarian ski resort of Borovetz. It was July, and most of the tourists staying at the hotel were Bulgarians fleeing the intense summer heat in Sofia. There were few foreigners around, and Ani wanted to take every opportunity to practice her English. The interview I had with her lasted twice as long as those I conducted with most other employees in the resort; she was eager to share all of her thoughts with me as long as I agreed to correct her grammar and pronunciation along the way.

Our interview was about labor in the tourism industry. I asked her a series of questions about working conditions, job satisfaction, and hopes for the future. Toward the end of every interview I usually turned to questions about the transition from communism to capitalism and what people remembered about it. Most of my interviewees were older. They had very clear recollections of the chaos and hardship that had characterized the last decades of their lives (with the notable exception of Damiana who saved all of her ire for the Bulgarian Communists). Many of my interviewees spoke of food shortages and ration coupons in the early 1990s, about not being able to find milk for their children. Others lamented the savings they lost when the banks collapsed, agonizing over the irony that those with the most debt were the true winners of the hyperinflation. Then there were the many men and women who feared unemployment, worrying about the lack of jobs once the old socialist factories started closing down. One woman talked at length about the crime and violence; her son had been shot and paralyzed from the waist down during a mafia shootout in a Sofia nightclub. He had been a professional soccer player. The general zeitgeist of the transition of 1989 was one of despair tempered by hope that things would soon start to get better.

In my interviews my favorite questions to ask were: "what was your first memory of the end of communism?" and "when was the first moment you realized that it was really over?" Given that Ani was so young in 1989, I imagined that she might not recall the exact moment when she became aware of the transition. I only decided to ask her the question because she was a Turk. In December 1984 the government of Bulgaria began something called the "rebirth" process, a program that forced the Turks of Bulgaria to give up their Turkish names and accept Slavic-sounding ones along with a series of other heavy-handed measures aimed at erasing the Turkish ethnicity from Bulgaria. Tensions between the Turkish minority and the Bulgarian government rose steadily throughout the late 1980s. Beginning in May 1989 the Bulgarian government began issuing exit visas to the ethnic Turks who refused to be assimilated, a signal that the Turkish minority was expected to leave Bulgaria at once. Many Turks were given only twenty-four hours to flee the country. By November 1989, when the Zhivkov regime finally fell after thirty-five years in power, over three hundred thousand Turks had fled, leaving behind their homes and possessions.

This expulsion was ironically called the Great Excursion, because the Bulgarian Communist Party tried to make it sound as if the Turks had left of their own free will. Although there were undoubtedly those who did, there were far more who left because they expected that the state would kick them out by force anyway. Because Turkey was a NATO-allied country, the Bulgarians feared Turkish aggression and irredentism. The government believed that expelling the Turks would prevent future Turkish intervention in Bulgaria's affairs. I guessed that Ani would remember those events even if she was only nine years old at the time.

Furthermore, the Bulgarian Turks were Muslims. Like Communists in other Eastern Bloc countries, the Bulgarian leaders believed that religion kept people from accepting modern life and the values associated with it, especially the equality of men and women in society. In Bulgaria headscarves and specific Islamic garments had been banned as well as the most intimate Islamic rituals: circumcision, Islamic burial practices, and the ability of Muslims to give their children Muslim names. I guessed from Ani's conservative attire that her family might be a devout one that suffered from religious persecution before 1989. I therefore assumed that she would have a far more critical view of the communist period than some of my other informants who had already begun to look back at it with considerable nostalgia.

Her answer surprised me. Our conversation captured the essence of what so many different Bulgarians had tried to articulate in different ways. Perhaps because Ani saw the Changes through the eyes of a child, she was able to distill into one small anecdote an entire universe of conflicting emotions and frustrations about the continued failures and social upheavals of the 1990s. She was able to put her finger on the one thing she felt had been lost in the transition.

"That is a difficult question because I was so young. Maybe in the third or fourth grade," she said, curling her hand and lifting it up to her mouth as she

A third-grade class photo from 1976.

searched for some remnant of a fingernail. She gnawed at a small piece of nail on her left ring finger for several moments, gazing up at the ceiling as she rustled around in her mind for the memory, a memory that seemed to be eluding her. Ani finally tore off a thin white sliver, exposing a raw, pink nail bed that looked like it was about to start bleeding.

"But I remember," she said at last. "One day our teacher came to class. And she told us that we should no longer call her Drugarkata Stefanova. Do you know the word *drugar*?"

"It means *comrade*, right?"

"Yes, *comrade*, but also *companion* or *friend*. And it could also mean *workmate* or *classmate*. Like a *colleague*," Ani said in careful English.

"That's what the Communists preferred to call each other: *comrades*?"

"Yes, but we all used that word. We were all *drugari* to each other," Ani explained, using the plural of the word in Bulgarian. She put her hand back up to her mouth once more, but before she could begin nibbling she paused and said, "Yes. I remember that one day our teacher, Drugarkata Stefanova . . . you know at that time we called all of our teachers drugar. And you know that *drugarka* is a woman drugar?"

"Yes," I said, "The feminine version of the noun?"

"Yes, but you don't have many gendered nouns in English."

"No, we don't. I make mistakes in Bulgarian all the time."

"We don't have gender nouns in Turkish either. It is curious how languages can be so different."

A Bulgarian "Happy Spring" card from the early 1970s. These were school photos that were sent to family and friends.

"Very curious," I said, trying to bring her back onto the topic. "You were telling me about Comrade Stefanova."

"Oh yes. Well, one day our teacher comes to class and tells us that we are no longer allowed to call her Drugarkata Stefanova. From now on we are supposed to call her Gospozha Stefanova, you know, like Lady Stefanova."

"Like Mrs. Stefanova?"

"That's right. Mrs. Stefanova. And we all thought it was very funny, because it made her sound so old, and she was really just in her twenties maybe. We kept calling her drugarka, or Mrs. Drugarka. She kept correcting us. Eventually she got very angry and told us that she was no longer our comrade but our teacher, and out of respect for her position we should call her missus."

"And why did that make such an impression on you?" I said.

"Well, it's because I don't remember much about communism. Because I was so young. But I do remember that we all called each other drugar. You see, because we students were drugari to each other, and we were drugari to our teachers and to other adults. And people in all sorts of different professions and living in different places, well, they were all drugari to each other, too. Everyone was a drugar."

She paused, sucking on a fingertip now that the last of her nails was gone. "When Drugarkata Stefanova told us to call her Gospozha, I realized for the first time how much everything was going to change. I had heard the rumors. I knew that my father was no longer afraid to listen to the American and British radio stations, and that there would be elections, and that Todor Zhivkov had gone away. But none of that meant anything to me. It did not affect me. Having to call my teacher missus, you know, which sounds so formal and like she is someone really important, that was the first thing to change in my life. So that's why I remember it."

"I see."

"And you know. It is because I very much liked the word *drugar*. There was something good about having one word for everybody. I don't remember too much about communism, but I do remember the word *drugar*. It is a good word: *drugar*," she said, heaving a deep sigh.

I nodded, scribbling down her words as fast as I could in my notebook.

"*Comrade* was a good word," she repeated, rolling the English-language version of it around on her tongue, emphasizing the r just slightly. "Comrade. Colleague. Friend. Maybe it was not really true, but I like to think that there *was* once a time when all Bulgarians, even Turks, were drugari to each other. I don't know. Maybe we lost something really important when we lost the word *drugar*."

CHAPTER 8   **PETAR HAILS A CAB**

He had just been offered a job in London. Petar immediately called his best friend and left the office to get a drink. It was a very good offer. Better than he could have hoped for. But he wanted to be talked out of taking it.

Petar walked out of the office complex in Mladost, a neighborhood in the eastern part of Sofia. It was a hot Tuesday in mid-July, and he was looking forward to a few weeks on the Bulgarian seaside beginning on the third of August. Petar worked for a small Bulgarian information technology company and was a member of the newly emerging middle class of young professionals who were still in primary school when the communist era ended in 1989. He had a steady salary and owned his own apartment in the center of town that he shared with his girlfriend, a journalist for a satellite radio station. On this particular Tuesday, Petar walked out into the blazing afternoon sun and headed down to the main boulevard where he could hail a taxi that would take him into the center of Sofia.

Petar was tall with striking Slavic good looks. Fine boned and blond with perfectly upright posture, he was the rare kind of Bulgarian man who watched his weight and did not smoke. He liked his whiskey neat and only drank *rakiya* on special family holidays when his mother forced him to. He ironed his shirts with heavy starch and spent fifteen minutes polishing his brown leather work shoes each morning before he left his flat. At twenty-eight, the hair on his head was starting to thin; he fastidiously avoided hats even in the freezing months of January and February, convinced that they would accelerate his inevitable baldness.

Petar had attended the best English-language secondary school in Sofia and had won a full scholarship to study for his bachelor's degree at the American University in Bulgaria, about two hours to the south in Blagoev-grad. He studied English for two years, but computers were his real passion. In his junior year he went on an exchange program to Stanford University in the United States, where he switched his major to computer engineering. He won another fellowship to complete his degree at Stanford with the support of a young assistant professor with whom he had done an independent study. This was the late 1990s, and it took less than a week for Petar to find a job in Silicon Valley upon graduation. With his H-1B visa arranged by his employer, Petar rented an apartment in Mountain View and began living the American dream: stock options, company vacations, Christmas bonuses, and more money than he could spend.

He lived for three years in California, but he slowly grew tired of the traffic and the gold-digging American girls named Mandy, Sandy, or Candee who swarmed him whenever he went for a drink at the local Applebee's. These women could smell the tech dorks the minute they walked into the restaurant, hoping to land a husband with a few hundred thousand in stock options. Petar had missed Sofia and had used his two-week vacation each year to go home to his parents and friends. He stayed in the United States only for the money. He knew there was no way he would be able to earn as much at home in Bulgaria.

It almost came as a relief when he was laid off in December of 2001. On his H-1B visa he had thirty days to find another job before he would be deported. But with thousands of other IT workers losing their jobs after the dot-com crash, Petar knew it was hopeless. He watched as his coworkers were forced to liquidate all of their possessions before boarding the plane back home—their options now worthless, and their once soaring net worth now evaporated. Petar also lost his stock options, but he had managed to save a good chunk of his salary.

Silicon Valley in the late 1990s had been a land of immigrants: Indians, Russians, Chinese, and Bulgarians, too. But Petar had never felt at home in the United States. The life was too fast, the people were too uncultured, and the women were all too big for his taste. More importantly, Petar was a Bulgarian, and he liked being a Bulgarian. In the United States Petar cooked Bulgarian food and listened to Bulgarian music, but it was never the same as being back in Sofia where he could walk into a bar and know half of the patrons by name. He happily left California to return home.

The problem was finding a job. Despite his degree from Stanford and his three years of experience in Silicon Valley, no one was willing to hire him for more than three hundred dollars a month. In America he had earned almost seven thousand dollars a month, and it was an insult to be offered so little money. Furthermore, he had idealized his country while he was away, not listening when his friends complained about the armed robberies, the corrupt traffic police, and the predatory municipal bureaucracy.

"Petar, you are an idiot for coming back," his friends said. "There is nothing for someone like you here."

Over a million young Bulgarians like Petar had fled the country in the 1990s, hoping to find better fortunes abroad. Many of Bulgaria's postcommunist difficulties were exacerbated by this huge brain drain of young and able men and women to the United States and Western Europe. The Bulgarian media endlessly lamented the migration situation, and beginning in 1997 the government started to actively encourage young Bulgarians to return home. The population was shrinking precipitously, and a United Nations prediction warned that by 2050 ethnic Bulgarians would no longer be a majority in their own country. With more and more young people of childbearing age leaving the country, it was only going to get worse.

"I am Bulgarian, and Bulgaria is my country," Petar would routinely pronounce after a few whiskeys, his nationalism sufficiently lubricated for the evening. "Someone has to be the first to stay, and it might as well be me."

Petar lifted his arm and waved at the oncoming traffic, hoping to find an empty cab. He had told his friend to meet him at the bar By the Way in twenty minutes. The late afternoon traffic would be heading out of, rather than into, the center of Sofia; it would be a quick ride. A few taxis sped by, a small red light signaling that they were occupied. Petar scanned the distant cars for a taxi with a green light. After several moments, Petar was still standing on the side of the boulevard with his arm extended. His thoughts started to wander to the job in London and what it would be like to have a real salary again, to be paid what he thought he was worth.

Lost in his thoughts, he did not notice when a taxi signaled and pulled over to pick him up. He glanced at the front hood of the cab. In big blue letters was the word *OK*, and he hopped into the passenger seat beside the driver without a second thought. The OK Supertrans taxi company was the biggest taxi company in Sofia. Their cars had a distinct look to them: bright yellow, royal blue lettering, and the phone number "2121" painted on their side doors. They charged reasonable rates: 0.59 stotinki per kilometer and 0.18 stotinki for each minute of waiting in traffic. He traveled in these taxis frequently, since Petar's Bulgarian salary did not allow him the luxury of his own car. Petar had used all his savings from the United States to buy his small apartment so he would not have to live with his parents like most of his friends did.

"Corner of Vassil Levski and Rakovsky," Petar said.

The driver pressed a button on the meter and sped off toward the center of town.

Petar had to admit to himself that the last three years in Bulgaria had been a disappointment. He had been unemployed for six months before taking a poorly paid job as a programmer. Despite the low wages the boss of that first company rarely paid salaries on time, and Petar had once gone three months without receiving compensation. He eventually quit and had tried to find a job with a Western firm in Bulgaria. It was almost impossible to find work like that without personal connections. The firms had Western bosses, but Bulgarians did all the hiring. Petar sent his resume into firms but never received replies. His girlfriend told him that he had to be introduced personally to someone in the firm if he wanted them to look at his materials, no matter how much experience he had. At one firm the Bulgarian human resources manager had actually asked him to pay a bribe to have his application forwarded to the hiring committee. "This is just like communism," Petar complained to his girlfriend.

Eventually Petar found work as a website designer for a German import and export firm for eight months. Then the German owner learned that his Bulgarian accountant had embezzled two hundred thousand euros. When he tried to take the accountant to court, the German received an anonymous death threat and had his nice Boyana home broken into and vandalized. The owner fired the entire staff, closed the firm, and vowed never to do business with Bulgarians again.

At last Petar found work at a local start-up that sold access to a database of Bulgarian public tax records. The two owners were young Bulgarians who had worked in the United States and hoped to start a business at home. But they had not sold as many subscriptions as they had hoped. Their humble revenue stream prevented them from raising Petar's salary even after a full year. The owners always paid him on time, but he simply could not live the life he wanted on five hundred leva a month. Sofia was an expensive city. He had searched for other work, but no one was willing to pay him more.

Still, London would be more expensive than Sofia. The British firm paid well, but it would also cost him a lot more to live. And he would be an immigrant again. Another East European laborer forced to make a living abroad because his country was so screwed up. "If you don't like it here, then go home," the Brits would tell him. And how different would he be from all the Bulgarian nannies, construction workers, cleaning ladies, and prostitutes "guest working" in the West?

As the taxi wove its way through the light traffic, Petar stared out the window. The grass on the side of the road was overgrown and full of weeds. The Municipality of Sofia had long since stopped tending to the public areas. The apartment buildings on either side of the street were a mix of colorful new high-rises sprouting up in between communist-era housing blocs with gray, crumbling facades. Packs of stray dogs roamed the sidewalks and dilapidated playgrounds, sniffing around the dumpsters that overflowed with heaps of rotting trash. Horse-drawn wooden carts driven by Romani families clattered from trash heap to trash heap looking for recyclables and discarded treasures.

The government had sold the waste disposal concession for the capital city to a private company owned by the Bulgarian mafia. They charged the municipality for cleaning the whole city but then only cleaned a few sections of it or picked up the trash only half of the time that they were supposed to. The snow removal concession had also been sold to a private company owned by local mobsters, so the streets of Sofia were only rarely cleared in the winter months, and then only in the very center of the city where the politicians lived and worked. It was a well-known way of transferring taxpayers' money from the state budget into the hands of wealthy elites. Everyone knew that the politicians were taking kickbacks from the trash collection and snow removal firms. Every year children got sick from the trash, and old people broke bones in the snow. But what could anyone do about it? They could vote the old politicians out of office. They would be

Trash on Vitosha Street, an exclusive shopping area in Sofia.

replaced by a new set of politicians that would probably do exactly the same thing. It could seem hopeless.

But this was his country. This was where he grew up and where his parents and parents' parents had grown up. This was where he kissed his first girl (Lyudmila with the red hair in the second grade) and where he learned to drive in his uncle's old beige Lada. This was the only country where they spoke his language, where he didn't always have to translate proverbs or explain idiomatic expressions. He knew the streets in Sofia without having to look at a map. He even knew all of the new names of the old streets whose names had been changed because they had sounded too communist; streets named after famous revolutionaries, like Vladimir Lenin, disappeared and new streets named after Bulgarian industrialists like Evlogi Georgiev appeared. Petar never understood why they had to change the names of the streets. Why should a change in politics change the way people found their way around the city? Had the British ever changed the names of streets in London, Petar wondered. It didn't matter, he would not know his way around them anyway. Sofia, despite everything, was home.

The taxi slowed and pulled up to a corner. Petar instinctively reached

A fake OK taxi in Sofia, which looks just like a real OK taxi.

down into his pocket for his wallet. He did this taxi ride almost ten times a week and knew that it would cost about six leva. He pulled a ten leva bill out of his wallet. He always tipped taxi drivers well. He knew that it was hard for them, too.

The taxi stopped. Petar glanced down at the meter. It read 29.26.

"Your meter is broken," Petar said, handing the driver the ten leva bill.

"Thirty leva," the driver said.

"Excuse me?"

"Thirty leva," said the driver, pointing at the sticker in the front right corner of his windshield.

Petar's eyes followed the driver's finger. On the mandatory window sticker listing the taxi rates, Petar saw that the standard OK rate of 0.59 was replaced by 2.59 and the 0.18 was replaced by a 1.18.

"But this is an OK taxi," Petar said.

"OK Superlux."

"What?"

"OK Superlux," the driver said, pointing once again at the window sticker. His voice was low and threatening.

Petar looked carefully at the sticker. The font of the letters was the same and the OK logo was the same. It looked exactly like a regular OK taxi sticker except that the rates had been changed. Upon closer inspection, however, Petar noticed that the word *Supertrans* had been replaced by *Superlux* and that the familiar "2121" phone number had a prefix of 873 painted in miniscule numbers in front of it. Petar looked around the cab; it looked exactly like a regular OK taxi.

"What is superlux about this?" Petar demanded.

"The rate is clearly posted on the window," the driver explained. "You entered into a contract with me when you got into my car. There is nothing illegal here."

"That's bullshit!" Petar yelled and reached for the door handle. In an instant he heard the doors of the car click locked. He could not get out.

"Thirty leva," the driver growled.

Petar looked at the man. His teeth were crooked and his hair was greasy and streaked with long strands of gray. He was older than Petar but looked much tougher. The skin around his eyes was wrinkled, and he had two days worth of black and gray stubble on his thick square chin.

"This is a six leva ride," Petar insisted. "I take it every day."

"Today it is thirty," the driver stated simply. "The rate is clearly posted. You should have looked before you got in."

"But you are pretending to be an OK taxi!" Petar was growing frustrated. "You have a big *OK* painted on your hood. "

"The rates are clearly posted," the driver repeated. Petar understood that there was nothing he could say that would change the driver's mind. The guy drove around Sofia looking for suckers like him all day. He would keep Petar locked in the car until he paid.

Petar thought about punching the driver but stopped himself. It was only thirty leva. Not enough to really risk breaking his nose over. Petar was in good shape, but he was also quite sure that the driver was ready for a fight and probably had a knife. Maybe even a gun. Petar berated himself for not looking at the window sticker when he got into a cab. But how could he have known? The car looked exactly like a regular OK taxi. He felt his anger simmering in the pit of his stomach. Today of all days.

He pulled his wallet out and handed the driver thirty leva. The door locks unclicked. Petar opened the door and jumped out. The driver said "thank you" just as Petar said "asshole" and slammed the door shut as hard as he could, hoping it would break.

As the driver sped away, Petar shoved his hands in his pockets, walking toward the bar where his friend would be waiting. Let someone else play the hero, a voice inside Petar's head whispered. He would be taking that job in London after all.

Despite the many injustices and frustrations of living in Bulgaria, my fascination with Eastern Europe continued to grow stronger as I traveled more extensively through the region. I watched with increasing curiosity as each of the postsocialist nations forged their unique pathways toward democracy and free markets, diverging in some ways but remaining uncannily similar in others. In its 1997 *Human Development Report*, the United Nations Development Program found that poverty throughout the former communist countries had increased tenfold and that the human costs of transition had been incredibly high. By the year 2000 the majority of postsocialist countries had not achieved the quality of life that they had enjoyed before 1989. Although governments had changed in all of the countries of the region, in some cases multiple times, the growing pains of transition did not seem to be easing at all.

In 2004 the first wave of East European countries joined the European Union. Although Bulgaria and Romania should have been included in this group, their accession was delayed for fear that they were not yet ready to join the club. Although I closely followed the trajectories of other postsocialist countries, Bulgaria remained the focus of my research. I, like many Bulgarians, was perplexed by what it was Bulgaria had done so differently from its brother socialist countries. Why had the Europeans let countries like Poland and Hungary join but excluded all of the Balkan counties save for Slovenia? Some said it was a residual fear of the Yugoslav wars and the atrocities that had been committed in the name of nationalism. Other Bulgarians argued that it was because they were Eastern Orthodox Christians. Still others felt that it was just racism against southeastern Europeans. All of them were deeply disappointed. I was disappointed, too. My daughter was officially a Bulgarian citizen, and I had hoped that she would become a European Union citizen as well. Just a little bit longer, the EU told Bulgarians and Romanians, but the promise sounded hollow. Bulgarians had already been waiting for the bright, shining future for a very long time.

It was during these years that I returned to live in Bulgaria for an extended period of time once again. I felt that immersing myself even more deeply into Bulgarian society was the best way to understand how these changes were affecting ordinary people's lives. But this process of studying others by cultural immersion was not always easy. Indeed, one of the biggest challenges I faced when trying to do research in Eastern Europe was picking up my life and moving it overseas. In addition to the grant proposals and visa applications, there was always personal upheaval. When I first started doing fieldwork in Bulgaria I was an unencumbered graduate student with few possessions. By 2005, however, I was married and had a three-year-old daughter. I also owned a house, furniture, and two cars that needed to be rented, stored, or sold before I could leave for a year. The most difficult part of that move, however, was the relocation of my two basset hounds from Maine to Bulgaria.

Tosca and Porthos were relatively well-traveled city dogs, and Sofia is one of those European dog-loving cities. I thought it would be fine to bring them. There was simply no way I could have left them back in the States for a year. In addition to all my other packing and arrangements, I had to deal with extra veterinary visits, health certificates, and special reservations so the dogs could fly on the plane with us as live cargo. The arrangement was that the dogs would live in Sofia with Hristo while my daughter and I lived five hours to the south in Madan, a small city of about nine thousand people with a Muslim majority. Through the months of June and July, Juliana and I would travel up to Sofia on weekends and take the hounds on long strolls through the large wooded park in the center of the city. Free from their leashes, Tosca and Porthos loved to romp around the forest and frolic with the Bulgarian dogs. Aside from my constant fear that they would be at-

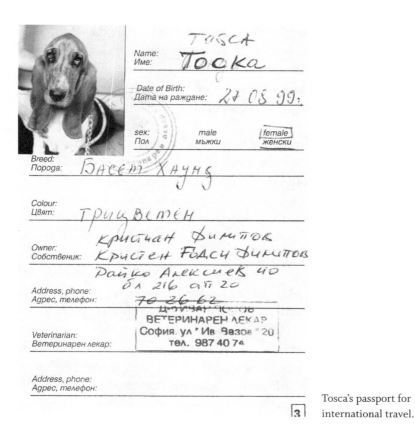

Name: Име:	*TOSCA* Тоска
Date of Birth: Дата на раждане:	2+ 05 99.
sex: Пол	male мъжки / female женски
Breed: Порода:	Басет Хаунд
Colour: Цвят:	Трикветен
Owner: Собственик:	Кристиан Димитов Кристен Годси Димитов
Address, phone: Адрес, телефон:	Дайко Алексиев 40 бл. 216 ап 20 70 26 62
Veterinarian: Ветеринарен лекар:	Д-р ЗАГ... ... ... ВЕТЕРИНАРЕН ЛЕКАР София, ул " Ив. Вазов " 20 тел. 987 40 7а
Address, phone: Адрес, телефон:	

|3| Tosca's passport for international travel.

tacked by one of the hundreds of stray dogs that roam the streets of Sofia, they settled into a happy routine.

In late August, however, business trips and other circumstances conspired so that there was no one available to watch the dogs in Sofia for seven days. That exact week also coincided with the annual summer festival in Madan that I did not want to miss. Why shouldn't I bring the bassets down to the field site? My daughter and I missed them, and they were always a conversation starter in Sofia. I had no reason to suppose that this would turn out to be a very bad idea.

The first problem was that my landlord needed some extra financial "reassurance" that the dogs would live out on the balcony and not inside the apartment. Second, basset hounds are very odd-looking dogs, famous in the United States for being the mascot of the Hush Puppies brand of shoes. They are long bodied with short stubby legs, droopy ears, sad bloodshot eyes, and loose wobbly flews. In Sofia most people thought the two hounds were adorable, but in Madan people were terrified. Wherever I walked them through town the locals gazed at them with horror. People stared at me as if I were walking two monsters through their streets: women fled from my path, children screamed, old grandmothers swore at me in muted Bulgarian.

A helpful neighbor suggested that I walk the dogs outside of town at the old soccer stadium. This seemed like the perfect solution. I would load the dogs into the car and drive them to the soccer field, overgrown with weeds and completely enclosed by dilapidated concrete bleachers. The first three times I took them there it was empty. Because it was enclosed, I could let them off their leashes to run through the tall grass with my daughter who chased them and squealed with delight. I would sit and watch them as they sniffed around, enjoying the fresh air and writing field notes in my journal about the day's events. Although my surroundings were sadly neglected and run down, I found it a peaceful place to think about all of the political and economic changes that had affected the people living in Madan.

When we arrived on the fourth day, Porthos and Tosca knew where they were going, and I let them out of the car without their leashes. Both dogs bounded happily toward the entrance. As my daughter and I slowly followed, I spotted, in the middle of the field, something that neither of my dogs had ever seen.

Sheep!

In the entranceway the female basset, Tosca, stood absolutely still, transfixed by about twelve sheep grazing no more than ten meters away in front of her. Her tail was straight up, her right front paw lifted, her long ears cocked forward. The sheep were riveting, and I could almost see the ancient canine urges swelling up in her chest. The only animals Tosca had ever met were other dogs, cats, and the occasional squirrel, but here in the flesh were relatively small white puffs of domesticated mammal that must have triggered some long forgotten hunting instinct buried under a lifetime of couch lounging and city life. With a bark as loud and deep as a sonic boom, Tosca set off at top speed toward the sheep, followed soon after by a baying Porthos.

The scene was thus: a dozen terrified sheep fleeing around the stadium, being followed by two fat dogs barking after them, being chased by a furiously shouting woman (me), being pursued by a wailing and confused toddler, being followed by two hysterical Bulgarian shepherdesses flailing their arms in dismay.

The sheep were faster than the dogs, but the dogs were much faster than me, so I ran across the field to try to cut them off. At that moment two men appeared: one of them was throwing large stones at Tosca and the other was running toward her with an axe. I was commanding Tosca to stop, but Tosca was so deep in the throes of her sheep fascination that she kept running. The sheep finally managed to jump out of the stadium, and a well-thrown rock walloped Tosca on her shoulder. She stopped just long enough so that I got to her before the axe-wielding man did.

The two men ran up to me, shouting about what the hell was I doing bringing dogs near the sheep. I breathlessly apologized and tried to explain that they had never seen sheep before.

"What do you mean they've never seen sheep? They are dogs!"

At this point, my daughter was howling with fear and the Bulgarian women were verbally assaulting me with curses. Before I could think of what I was saying, I blurted, "They are American!"

Of all of the things the men expected me to say, I do not think they were prepared for that. Both men immediately fell silent. They stared at each other. They stared at the hounds. They stared at me. In a region of Bulgaria where few people have ever left the province, let alone the country, the very idea of foreign dogs was absurd. But it was the only explanation I had. So I stuck to it.

"They are American dogs. They live in the city. They won't hurt the sheep, they are just curious."

"American dogs!" one of the men shouted, "American dogs?"

Puzzled at his own utterance of this remarkable revelation, he slowly lowered his axe. It was an awkward moment, and I could see that the men were waiting for further details.

It took over an hour to explain the path that brought my two basset hounds to this abandoned soccer stadium in one of the poorest, most isolated regions in the Balkans. The two men and two women asked me many questions: Did the dogs have passports? Were they American citizens? Did they need visas? Did they fly on the plane with us? Did they have their own seats? If Bulgaria joined the EU, would their animals be EU citizens, too? Would they get passports?

I was patient and described the many details of international dog travel, as well as why some Americans care so much about their pets and how dogs in the West were not just pets but often considered part of the family. The men watched with interest as my daughter hugged the now leashed dogs, gently caressing Tosca's back and cooing in her ear. I tried to explain that they were not citizens but enjoyed the privileges of their owner's citizenship.

Slowly, I realized how thoroughly wrong it had been to bring the dogs to Madan. I was deeply ashamed to realize that my two hounds enjoyed social and economic privileges systematically denied to these people, particularly in the wake of Bulgaria's postponed entrance into the EU. It must have been so insulting to them.

On the other hand, for about an hour on one day in August, Tosca and Porthos allowed these Bulgarians to become the ethnographers, forcing me to reflect upon and answer questions about the many peculiarities of my own cultural practices. I had suddenly become the object of study; they would not let me leave until all of their queries were answered. I was the first American they had ever met, and they had dozens of questions for me. As we parted that day, I knew that I had a great story, but I was certain they did, too. Despite the difference between us, they too were now in a position to become cultural translators. I was quite sure that the tale of the crazy American and her fancy mutant-looking dogs would be told among the shepherds of Madan for years to come.

CHAPTER 10

THE MASTER OF CONSPIRACIES, 2005

In that same summer of 2005 I often found myself in need of an office when I came up to Sofia. I could arrange for Internet access at home, but I also required a printer, scanner, and photocopier as well as a place to store my ever-growing library of research materials. By the mid-2000s, after a long struggle to get himself set up, Kaloyan had become a well-established entrepreneur. He owned one of the most successful public relations companies in Sofia and had settled into a comfortable life as one of the capital city's most eligible bachelors. His wife had permanently immigrated to the United States, and they were now officially divorced. He had a new girlfriend who had a PhD in sociology. She was smart in addition to being young and attractive. I liked Kaloyan even more for choosing an educated and intelligent woman when he could have chosen any bimbo in Sofia he wanted.

Kaloyan offered to let me share his office for the summer. I would pay a small fee for unlimited use of his printer and Xerox machine and would have an entire room with a large desk all to myself. His assistant, a young university student working toward her degree in physics, was named Desi. She was at work five days a week and helped me with all sorts of bureaucratic issues whenever they arose. Kaloyan, however, only spent a few hours in his office each day. He would roll in at about 10:00 a.m. and work for about three hours. At around 1:00 p.m. he would go out for a long lunch where he inevitably started drinking rum cocktails. After lunch he would meet potential clients in bars around the city, being the rainmaker for his firm. Apparently he was really good at this; he never seemed to have a shortage of clients. That was how business in Bulgaria was done. You had to drink with people if you wanted them to hire you.

On the days when I was not in Madan, I would drop off my daughter, Juliana, with her grandmother and spend long hours in Kaloyan's office reading online chats on a Bulgarian Islamic website. The site was an electronic forum for young Bulgarian Muslims to learn about the "proper" Islam from Saudi Arabia and Jordan. I often printed out long online discussions about whether or not women should wear the headscarf or if polygamy should be allowed in Bulgaria for Muslim minorities. Kaloyan thought it was weird that I would waste so much time reading these forums and was probably annoyed that I insisted on printing them all out. But he was always friendly to me and would sometimes take Desi and me out for lunch. He had a special table in a local restaurant where the waitresses all knew exactly what he wanted to eat and drink. After eating, we would sometimes hang out in the restaurant for hours talking about local politics now that my Bulgarian was good enough. Occasionally, we would migrate to another bar to meet Hristo for drinks. Wherever we ended up, Kaloyan would inevitably try to educate me about what was *really* going on in Bulgaria.

After six years of doing research on Bulgaria I had grown accustomed to the ubiquity of the conspiracy theory. It was not only Kaloyan. A favorite Bulgarian pastime was to sit around with friends and discuss who might secretly be pulling the strings behind the scenes. After hearing Hristo's story about Chernobyl I understood why Bulgarians were so mistrustful of everything, but I still took their stories with a huge grain of salt. I just wasn't the kind of person to believe that everything was smoke and mirrors. But Kaloyan was the best. He was the grand master of the conspiracy theory, a black belt in alternative narratives. I often found myself sitting around a table with a group of Bulgarians listening to him hold forth. I don't know where he got them all.

His favorite genre of theories had to do with corrupt privatization transactions and how the Bulgarian people had been robbed of billions of dollars of their collective wealth. Under communism all productive units in society—all industry, agriculture, and services—were owned by the state. The state was the only employer and owned the so-called means of production on behalf of the people. In other words, the wealth of the nation was collectively owned, but the caretaker of that wealth was the Bulgarian Communist Party (BCP). During the 1980s the BCP had mismanaged the economy and put the country into debt to Western creditors. After 1989 the Bulgarian government needed to sell off many of these collectively owned assets to foreign investors to raise hard currency to service these debts.

This was a messy business, and it is undeniable that the process could have been handled in a less chaotic fashion. Valuable enterprises were intentionally undervalued and sold for sums far less than they were worth, and certainly, elected politicians took bribes and kickbacks from different foreign bidders. And it was no secret that many once viable enterprises had been deliberately run into bankruptcy so that the foreign investor could sell it off in pieces, turn a quick profit, and get out of Bulgaria. But Kaloyan took the chaos of privatization to a whole new level, claiming that the Americans had installed the pro-Western government in 1997 with the understanding that the newly "elected" prime minister would guarantee that American companies were given preference in all of the most important privatization transactions.

"The problem was that the Bulgarians got greedy. They wanted some of the enterprises for themselves," Kaloyan said one evening. "So they double-crossed the Americans. That's why Kostov's government got booted out in 2001."

"Oh come on, Kaloyan. Are you saying that the Americans choose who wins and loses elections? Do you really think the CIA is that competent?"

"In the 1990s they did, yes," he said. "But then they lost control of it all."

"But those were free elections! Maybe the Americans gave campaign donations, but they wouldn't fix the elections."

"All elections are fixed in Bulgaria," he said, "because there is only one party running."

"What do you mean one party? There are seven different parties in parliament now."

"But they are all controlled by one party: the Rich Party."

I had known Kaloyan for a long time. I knew that once I got him started on the conspiracy theories I would have to be willing to hear him out. That could take a while, and I had to be in the right mood. On this particular evening, however, I had already had a few drinks, my husband Hristo was working late, and my daughter was safely ensconced at my mother-in-law's flat. I figured what the hell? No matter what he came up with, Kaloyan was always entertaining. The parliamentary elections had just happened, and the Bulgarian Socialist Party had won. Everyone in Sofia was talking about the results, and I was curious to hear Kaloyan's take on them. "The Rich Party?" I asked, inviting him to continue.

He smiled a wide, friendly grin and leaned in toward me.

"There is only one political party, just like there was before. The Communists were simple and just outlawed the opposition, but the 'democrats' are cleverer. They just buy the opposition."

"Who are the 'democrats?'" I asked.

"Oligarchs, mostly. Powerful men with money. It is like a big poker game," he explained. "Whoever can buy into the game is given a seat at the table. And they all benefit from the stupidity of the people. They control the entire political process. It doesn't matter which party you vote for, they are all controlled by the oligarchs."

"But how?"

"It is the perfect marketing scheme," he said, getting excited. "Let me give you an example. Let's say you come to me and you want to sell soap. You can make one type of soap that does the job of smelling nice and cleaning the dirt and oil off of your skin. It's a basic soap with nothing fancy about it, but it works fine. It's inexpensive to produce, and you can produce a lot of it. The problem is that everyone has to get the same kind, and people complain that they don't have any choices. That is communism."

He picked up a box of matches and set it down in front of me. "Now if you were clever, you could take the same soap and just make a few different versions of it. This happens in marketing all the time. You make a soap that is pink and smells like roses and write on the package that it is for dry skin. You make another that is purple and smells like lavender, and another is white and smells like coconut. You say that one is good for dry skin, one is good for oily skin, you know. You put a different naked woman on each package with some bullshit, and you give people a choice: pink, purple, or white. But it is still more or less the same soap, and the same company sells them all. Whether you buy the pink one or the white one, the same people get your money. That is democracy. In Bulgaria, we have socialists and Turks and nationalists and moderates, but they are all just different brands of the same product. With all power in their hands, the oligarchs can make the laws and set the policies that will best preserve their wealth."

A poster for a nationalist political party, which reads "Support Ataka, Save Bulgaria."

"So you are saying that these political parties are all manufactured?"

"Sure. The king's party came out of nowhere in 2001, and Ataka just suddenly appeared this summer. And you know how easy it is to buy votes." Kaloyan had a point there. Just months before the parliamentary elections in 2001, Bulgaria's former tsar created a political movement with no clear platform and won the election in a landslide. A month or so before the 2005 elections, a new nationalist party appeared out of the blue and won twenty-one seats in parliament, forcing an unwieldy three-way coalition government. And the rumor (later confirmed) was that all of the major political parties paid up to fifty leva in cash if you took a picture of your ballot with your mobile phone and could prove that you had voted for their party.

"But if that were all true," I said, "why even bother having a parliament at all? Why bother with elections?"

"It's political theatre to keep the West happy. If you haven't noticed, not being democratic enough can get you invaded." He was referring to the wars in Iraq and Afghanistan and George W. Bush's aspirations for bringing democracy to the Middle East. "Besides, it's easier to control people if they think they actually have a say in choosing their government. There is not just one party to blame. It's the whole system, and it's much harder to take a system down, especially when those who control that system have all of the wealth."

"But think of the cover-up this would require. Surely, there would be some kind of paper trail," I said. It was plausible that Bulgaria's political parties all accepted campaign donations from the same businessmen; that happened everywhere. But Kaloyan was suggesting that the oligarchs in Bulgaria actually created political parties to run in sham elections just to keep the West happy. This seemed ridiculous to me. It was just too far fetched. "And if even a fraction of what you say is true, why isn't anyone writing about it? The press would be all over it."

"What press? You think they don't control that, too?"

Oh no. I had opened another can of worms. Kaloyan was agitated now. His business was public relations, and he knew the media business in Bulgaria very well. And the so-called free press was a touchy subject with many Bulgarians I knew. In the early 1990s Bulgaria went from having a handful of state-owned newspapers that they knew to be filled with government propaganda to having literally hundreds of newspapers and news sources with different political points of view trying to make sense of the chaos of the transition. Throughout the first decade of the transition, there was allegedly a price list for how much it would cost to purchase a "news" story on the front page of every major newspaper in Bulgaria.

"You think they are just propaganda for the Rich Party? That journalists are paid to write articles?" I said.

"Oh no, they are paid *not* to write articles," he said.

"What?"

"Do the math," Kaloyan said, crushing one cigarette into a Havana Club promotional ashtray and instantly lighting another. "All you have to do is find out what their production costs are. How much to produce the paper, how many staff journalists they have, the rent for their editorial offices, etcetera. Then you calculate how much they are charging for each issue and how much they charge for advertising. Just flip through a week's work of their papers and you can easily calculate how much advertising revenue they are taking in. If you know their circulation, you can figure out how much they take in from newsstand sales. They will also have a small revenue stream from the classified section. Most of the major Bulgarian dailies charge less than one leva per issue and have limited circulation, which means that they are not making enough money to break even. They are operating at a loss."

"So why don't they go bankrupt?" I asked.

"Racketeering or foreign governments. Investigative journalists will go out and write stories about famous people or politicians, usually negative ones about corruption or sensitive personal issues. The people will pay the newspapers not to run the stories. The only paper that prints the real scandals is *Weekend*, the tabloid. All the others are paid off. The papers are racketeering the politicians, so the people never know what is really going on."

"Unless you read *Weekend*," I joked.

"Yes. *Weekend* is the only free press in Bulgaria."

"So what do foreign governments have to do with this?"

"Well, there are some papers . . ." Kaloyan said, taking a long drag on his cigarette and then exhaling slowly up toward the wood paneled ceiling. "There are some papers that do not accept advertising or are very selective in what products they will advertise. For instance, there are some papers I do not even try for my campaigns because they do not rely at all on advertising revenue. They charge very high rates. Foreign governments bankroll these papers. For a long time it was the Americans and sometimes the British. But mostly the Americans. They gave a lot of money to promote the free press, but mostly they were propping up pro-American papers. Now it is more likely to be the Russians. I think *Vestnik Ataka* [the nationalist newspaper] gets money from the Russians. And of course, all of the Turkish language newspapers and magazines get money directly from the Turkish government. They don't even hide that. Everyone knows that."

"So let me get this straight," I said, trying to put all the pieces together in my mind. "There is an amorphous group of businessmen who secretly control all of the political parties in Bulgaria and who pay voters to go to the polls in sham elections so that they can fool the West into thinking that Bulgaria is a democracy. They control the government and pass laws that will protect and increase their wealth."

He nodded.

"And they use the media as a tool to blackmail the politicians into not complaining about this arrangement."

"Exactly," he said.

"And they let the foreign governments in because . . . ?"

"Because they are not a threat. If they become a problem, the oligarchs will just shut them down."

"And you know about this because . . . ?"

"Because I think," Kaloyan said. "Do you think the Communists went away? Some of them are still here, together with the new mafia bosses and the big businessmen. Those people are in control of everything in Bulgaria, just like before 1989. Only now they have learned to do it more effectively."

"Where do you get this stuff?" I asked, laughing. "You should write a book."

Kaloyan sat back in his chair and used a long plastic stirrer to swirl the ice around in the bottom of his now empty mojito. I wondered how much of this he actually believed or if he just liked talking about it. He was a smart, educated, and successful entrepreneur, and his description of Bulgaria didn't seem to jive with his own experiences. Still, talking about the conspiracy theories always gave me an interesting window into how Bulgarians were thinking about the pros and cons of the transition. And Kaloyan was really the best. Maybe I should write an article? Or maybe just collect some of the best theories I had heard over the years and publish them on their own. Kaloyan would be the perfect source.

"You have so many different ideas about what's going on in Bulgaria, Kaloyan. Tell me, what's the best conspiracy theory you ever heard?" I asked, stumbling over the Bulgarian words for *conspiracy theory*.

He looked at me as if I had not been listening to him at all. When he spoke it was slowly and deliberately.

"There are no 'conspiracy theories' in Bulgaria," he said. "They are all true."

CHAPTER 11

AN EXPLOSION IN SOFIA, 2008

It was around 6:30 a.m. when I heard the explosion. It was the third of July, and I had an early flight from Sofia to Berlin to give a lecture at the Einstein Forum and to attend a reception at the grand reopening of the United States Embassy on Pariser Platz for the Fourth of July. It was now nineteen years since the fall of the Berlin Wall, and the new American Embassy would be right in the shadow of the Brandenburg Gate. I was nervous about the talk and had slept rather badly, finding it hard to shut off the incessant chatter in my head and obsessing about whether to wear a suit or a dress to the reception. At some point close to 5:00 a.m. I had finally drifted off into a deep sleep. My alarm was set for 7:00 a.m. Two hours of really good-quality sleep would have been enough. And then . . .

BOOM!

I literally jumped out of bed at the sound, my heart pounding. It was so loud. My ears immediately started ringing. Thousands of car alarms were activated at once, adding a cacophony of high-pitched screeches to punctuate my panic. The stray dogs went crazy, barking wildly. I looked out the window of my seventh story apartment to see if I could figure out what had caused it. Everything looked normal. For a moment I thought that it was thunder, but the sky was blue and there was no sign of a storm anywhere on the horizon.

That was a bomb, I thought to myself. A bomb has just gone off.

I turned the television on and flipped through the channels to find some news, but there were no reports as of yet. I was alone in the apartment. I grabbed my cell phone and called my now ex-husband who was sleeping across town with our now six-year-old daughter. It was early, but I figured he had to have heard the blast. Perhaps he knew what was going on.

"Hello." His voice did not sound groggy at all even though it was 6:30 a.m. and I knew he was not going to wake up until 7:00 a.m.

"Are you okay? Is everything okay? Is Juliana okay?"

"Yes. Everything is fine. She is still sleeping."

"Sleeping? Didn't you hear the explosion?"

"Yeah. It woke me up, but she managed to sleep through it."

"What the hell was that?"

"I don't know. But it's probably nothing."

"It was really loud. It sounded like a bomb."

"Yeah. Probably some car bomb went off in a mobster's jeep. Don't worry about it. It's probably nothing."

"You'll be here at eight, right?"

"Yeah. No problem, we'll take you to the airport."

Knowing that my daughter was safe and that she had managed to sleep through the blast put my mind at ease. Hristo was probably right; this would not be the first car bomb mafia killing in Bulgaria. His brother had once only narrowly avoided a car accident after an exploding mafia car had taken out a good chunk of the road between Sofia and Samokov. I took a deep breath and went to take a shower, leaving the television on in case there was any news.

BOOM!

At 6:45 a.m. there was another one, not as loud as the first but still loud enough to set off another round of wailing car alarms and to make me run dripping out of the shower to the phone. I called Hristo again.

"Did you hear that one?"

"Yeah. I don't know what the hell is going on." Now he sounded a little worried.

"Is Juliana still sleeping?"

"No, she woke up this time."

"There is nothing on the news."

"Yeah, I know. Go ahead and get ready. I'll call you if I see anything."

I hung up the phone and went back into the shower to rinse the conditioner out of my hair. After wrapping myself in a towel, I flipped through the channels one more time. There was still no news. I turned on my computer and went to the Focus News Agency website, a Bulgarian press service. The top story read that explosions had been heard in Sofia, but the source of the explosions was not yet known. The government had not issued any statements. Was it a mafia killing? Was the capital being bombed? Was it a terrorist attack? This last thought stopped me in my tracks. It might be a terrorist attack. That seemed to make a lot of sense. There had been bombings in London, Madrid, and Istanbul, and it was perfectly plausible that they might also hit Sofia.

I walked back into the bedroom to get dressed. A few moments later I heard an anchorperson on the Bulgarian National Television station confirm that residents of Sofia had been awakened at 6:28 a.m. by a deafening explosion, but there was still no information about what had caused the blast. Over the next hour the news station scrambled to figure out what was going on. It slowly became apparent that the blast had come from a munitions depot in Chelopechene, a village just outside of Sofia. The first explosion had been so strong that it blew the windows out of nearby houses and snapped several trees in half. The second explosion I heard was now being followed by a series of smaller explosions. I flipped the channel and saw images of residents fleeing their homes in a panic, hysterical over the damage and choking on the smoke. Fire trucks and ambulances rushed to the scene, but there was little they could do since the smaller explosions had not yet stopped. Some residents from Chelopechene claimed that they had seen a mushroom cloud form over the munitions depot and feared that there had been a nuclear explosion.

"Oh shit!" I said to myself.

I switched the channel again and saw a journalist accompanying some sort of scientist who was checking the air for radiation with a Geiger counter. He assured the journalist that there was no radiation detectable in the air, but he could not test for the residue of chemical weapons. I took a deep breath and tried to calm myself with the knowledge that Bulgaria did not have any nuclear weapons during the Cold War. But it did have chemical weapons.

"Why isn't the government saying anything?" I said to the TV, trying to squelch the panic rising in my stomach. I thought about my little daughter and wished for a moment that we had just stayed home in Maine for the summer.

I thought about calling Hristo a third time and telling him to get the hell out of town with Juliana. My phone rang.

"Hello?"

"There was an explosion at a munitions depot."

"I know," I said, "I'm watching the news, too."

"I don't think it is anything to worry about," Hristo said, knowing that I would be very nervous about leaving for Berlin under these circumstances. "We'll be over to pick you up in ten minutes."

"They are saying that there could be chemical weapons."

"No, people are just paranoid. They have checked the air, and there is no radiation."

"But what about chemicals? There could be chemicals."

"Calm down, Kristen. It's nothing. It's just an accident. There are no chemicals. It is just conventional stuff."

"How do you know for sure? Why isn't the government saying anything?" I asked. I was really starting to freak out.

"Because they are a bunch of incompetent idiots!" Hristo snorted.

"Right," I exhaled. "You're right. Okay. See you in ten minutes. I'll wait for you downstairs."

I finished getting ready and went down to wait in front of the apartment block. The car alarms had all stopped and everything seemed back to normal. Sofia residents were hurrying off to work as if it were any regular Thursday morning. No one around me seemed to be in much of a panic. This calmed me. I was overreacting. Everything would be fine. My daughter was safe.

When they came to get me, I climbed into the back seat of the taxi with Juliana and rode next to her to the airport.

"Mommy, did you hear the 'splosion?"

"Yes, sweetie. It was really loud. But it is all over now."

"Do you have a bye-bye present for me?" she asked.

"Yes," I said, thankful to change the subject. "But you won't get it until I have to go through security."

"What is it?"

"You'll see when you get it."

We made it to the airport in less than ten minutes. I went directly to the counter, checked my bags, and collected my boarding pass.

"Gate A5," said the agent cheerfully. "Please be at the gate thirty minutes before departure."

I spent the next forty minutes drinking outrageously overpriced coffee at the airport café with Hristo and Juliana. I was already starting to get nervous about my lecture, which I would be giving later that afternoon in Potsdam. Some of the earlier flights had been delayed, but everything else seemed normal. When the time came, I stood up and kissed my daughter good-bye and gave her the small Playmobil toy that I had bought for her so she wouldn't cry as I left her. She was delighted and hugged my leg, saying "Thank you, mommy." I thanked Hristo and headed through security.

For international departures from the Sofia airport you go up an escalator to security and passport control. The security check is first, and then you proceed to several booths where the border police check your passport and let you into the departure area. I waved to Juliana as I traveled all the way up the escalator, and she shouted "Bye-bye, mommy," in her small, six-year-old voice.

At the X-ray machine I unpacked my laptop and put it into one tray. In another tray I put my purse and my plastic quart bag of liquids in bottles smaller than thirty milliliters. I took my shoes off, then my belt, and finally my jacket and dropped them into a third bin. Once through the metal detector, I was patted down by a female security guard. I had become accustomed to all of the extra security measures since September 11, 2001. I know that many people are afraid of flying and associate airports with danger and that the enhanced security was supposed to make me feel safer. Most of the time it just annoyed me. The rules seemed arbitrary and only selectively enforced.

After my frisking I collected my things. Laptop and liquids back into the bag, shoes, belt, and jacket back on. I hitched my purse over my shoulder and walked toward the immigrations booths. I was in the no-man's-land between security and immigration when it happened. I saw two policemen situate themselves in the spaces between the three booths and heard one of the policemen inform a woman in the booth to my far right that they were closing the airport. I was the only person stuck between security and the border control so I walked up to the nearest policeman and asked what was going on.

"You need to go back. The airport is now closed."

"Why?"

"The airport is now closed," he repeated.

I immediately fumbled through my purse for my cell phone and called Hristo.

"Where are you?" I said.

"We are waiting for a taxi."

"Wait for me," I said. "They are closing the airport. I don't think my flight is going to leave."

The personnel at the security station tried to stop me, telling me that I could not go back out. I pointed to the policeman behind me. "He told me to go this way. He said the airport is closed."

The man at the metal detector exchanged some words with my policeman, and they agreed to let me through. I took the escalator back down to the check-in area and was soon joined by my daughter and ex-husband.

For the next forty-five minutes we tried to figure out what was going to happen with my flight. I had a Lufthansa ticket, so I went first to the Lufthansa ticket counter. The German man behind the desk looked exasperated. He was cradling a phone between his ear and his shoulder and typing into a computer.

He looked at my ticket. "Your flight is operated by Bulgaria Air," he said, pointing to a long line in front of a desk five counters down to his left. "You'll have to check there for rebooking information."

"What's going on?" I asked.

"The military has closed the airport."

"Why?"

"We don't know."

"For how long?"

"They won't tell us. Until further notice."

Without knowing when they were going to reopen the airport, I had no choice but to go stand in the long Bulgaria Air line to see about rebooking my ticket and getting my luggage back. The people in line around me were nervous. I heard two young men speaking in Bulgarian behind me.

"We should get out of here. They are closing the airport because there is going to be another explosion."

"But what if they reopen the airport and our flight leaves without us. What about our luggage?"

"My luggage is not worth my life. We should get out of here."

Ahead of me there was an attractive woman in her early forties speaking loudly into her mobile phone. "I don't know what is going on. They are closing the airport. No flights are taking off or landing. They are sending all arriving flights to Plovdiv. They are not telling us when they are going to reopen it. I am waiting in a long line. Maybe you should come pick me up?"

Plovdiv is Bulgaria's second largest city about 160 kilometers from Sofia. I looked out the window to check the weather, but it was a perfect July summer day.

I looked apprehensively over at Juliana playing with Hristo on a bench in the middle of the check-in area. The first man in the line behind me had convinced his friend to leave the airport. The woman on the mobile phone was looking very nervous. I looked around the airport and guessed that there were about three hundred people around the check-in area, and I assumed that there were many people that were stranded on the other side of the passport control. I heard someone else in line saying that Chelopechene was not far from the airport and that some windows had been broken in the initial blast this morning. I looked around the new airport and realized that the entire structure was made of glass. This would not be a safe place if there was another explosion. I was slowly working myself into a state of renewed panic when . . .

"GET OUT OF THE BUILDING NOW! GET OUT OF THE BUILDING IMMEDIATELY!"

Five uniformed policemen were shouting in Bulgarian in deep threatening voices. "GET OUT IMMEDIATELY!"

The Bulgarians around me started running toward the doors. The two women behind the Bulgaria Air counter stood up and fled. There were foreigners in the line looking very confused. I realized that they did not understand what was going on. No one was making any announcements in English.

"IZLIZAITE VEDNAGA!" The police were shouting in Bulgarian, waving people toward the doors.

"They are telling us to get out," I translated, "They are telling us to get out of the building!"

I saw raw fear in the eyes of a group of young British tourists who bolted immediately toward the doors. The police kept shouting in Bulgarian.

"IZLIZAITE VEDNAGA!"

Hristo had already scooped up our daughter, had grabbed my arm, and was dragging me toward the door; his painfully tight grip a testament to his own nerves. When we got out of the terminal we started walking as fast as we could toward the taxi rank. All of the taxis were already gone.

"Fuck!" Hristo shouted.

"Mommy, what's happening?"

"We have to get away from the airport, honey," I said. "The police are telling us to get away from the building."

"Why?"

"We don't know, sweetie. We just have to do what the police tell us. They are trying to keep us safe."

The three of us followed the crowd and started walking on the road that lead away from the airport and back into Sofia. Hristo put Juliana down and pulled out his phone. "I'll call Kaloyan to pick us up. He'll be at home now."

There was a steady stream of private cars whizzing by us on the road. Some of the Bulgarians had started running, which immediately had the effect of making everyone think that they needed to run too. I grabbed my daughter's hand and pulled her close to me, fearing that she might get knocked down. I turned around and faced the oncoming cars, sticking my thumb out in hopes that someone would stop and give us a ride.

"No one will stop!" Hristo said, punching numbers into his phone.

I did not care. I walked backward; dragging Juliana with me, with my thumb out hoping that someone would stop for the child. No one did. At least fifteen cars just sped by us, clearly panicked and unwilling to stop even for a moment.

"Come on," I pleaded as more frightened Bulgarians ran past us.

"Why is everyone running, mommy?"

"Never mind, honey. Just keeping walking with me."

"I'm telling you, Kristen, it is pointless," Hristo shouted.

I stepped out a little farther into the road. My eyes were now filling with tears of frustration, and I was thinking that if a car did not stop soon I would jump out in front of one and make them take my daughter into town. I was not thinking straight any longer. I was infected by the panic that surrounded me, amplified by a bad night's sleep, and finding myself in a life-and-death situation with my ex-husband, with whom my relationship was friendly but still rather awkward. He lived in Bulgaria and I lived in the United States, and we saw each other a few times a year because of Juliana. It would have been terribly ironic if we were going to die together after all.

"Kaloyan," he said, "we are at the airport, and there are no taxis. We need to get into Sofia. Can you pick us up?"

Just then I saw a large black jeep driving toward us. It was the kind of jeep that looked like it might have bulletproof glass for the windows. Mobsters, I thought. I stepped out a little further in the road, pulling Juliana with me and leaving Hristo a bit behind. I stuck my thumb out and caught the driver's eye, pleading with him silently for the sake of my daughter. Please stop. Please stop. Please, please, please stop.

He veered over to the side of the road. There were two men in the car. The one in the passenger seat flung open the door and barked, "Get in!"

I pulled open the back door and almost threw Juliana to the back seat. Hristo saw us and ran toward the Jeep. "Get in," I shouted, grabbing his arm as hard as he had grabbed mine in the terminal. I looked toward the driver and simply said, "her father" in Bulgarian. He nodded, and I climbed in after him and slammed the door. Before the door was even closed, the driver had pounded his foot on the gas, and we were out of the airport in less than two minutes speeding toward Sofia. My heart was about to explode, and my teeth seemed to be floating in a pool of adrenaline. I clutched the door handle on the back seat as the driver weaved in and out of the traffic.

The driver was a Ukrainian, probably a big mafia boss judging by the luxurious leather interior of his jeep and his ten thousand dollar Patek Phillipe watch. His passenger was a Bulgarian who traded a few sentences with Hristo about where we wanted to be dropped off. They were obviously not as unnerved by the situation as we were. I thanked them profusely in Bulgarian and in English, and if I could speak Swahili I would have thanked them in that language as well. I told the driver that he was a very good man, even though I suspected that he was probably a very, very bad man. I didn't care.

We were safe.

Hundreds of people were still stranded because they were not allowing either taxis or private cars to go near the terminal, so we were really lucky to get out. The military had declared martial law over the airport and would not even let airport personnel walk on the tarmac to retrieve the luggage that was already stored in the baggage holds.

I spent that whole day in a café with Juliana and Hristo hoping that the airport would reopen. I called my hosts in Germany to inform them that it was unlikely that I would make it for my talk that afternoon, although there was still no information about when flights would resume. We called friends and relatives to try to figure out what was happening, but no one knew any more than we did.

The explosions and the subsequent airport closure were never fully explained. The government launched an investigation, but there was some kind of high-level cover-up going on, because they never found a definitive cause for the initial explosion. There were no direct fatalities from the blast; the four guards at the depot escaped completely unharmed. What journalists managed to piece together afterward was that the munitions stored at the Chelopechene depot were Cold War–era conventional arms that the previous government had slated to be decommissioned.

There were a lot of weapons that should have been at Chelopechene. Someone in the Ministry of Defense had a list of the arms that had been sent there for decommissioning and realized that (according to the official inventory on file) the size of the first blast earlier in the morning was not enough to account for all of the munitions that were supposed to be there. If all of the inventory were in Chelopechene, as it was supposed to be, the military predicted that there would be a second blast that would have completely destroyed the Sofia Airport, possibly killing everyone inside. That is why the Ministry of Defense issued the order for the emergency evacuation of the terminal and took over the airport. The fact that there was no second catastrophic explosion was proof that the weapons that should have been there were no longer there.

Rather than decommissioning the arms, it was alleged that some high-level officials in the Ministry of Defense in the former government had been illegally selling them on the black market and pocketing the profits. The Bulgarian newspapers speculated that the explosion had been deliberately set off to cover up the amount of theft that had been going on at the depot. The initial explosion and the subsequent blasts fully destroyed all evidence that there had been illegal selling of weapons. Hundreds of passengers were stranded at the airport, many of them terrified that this was some kind of terrorist attack. Bulgaria would make the nightly news across Europe. But with the actual evidence now destroyed, there was no way anyone could prove that anyone had sold anything. No one was ever prosecuted or held responsible for the explosions.

But I would find out about all of that later. That morning I was terrified. Looking back, what I remember most about that day was the time I spent in the café with Hristo after we had fled the airport in the jeep. The excitement had tempered the awkwardness between us. I was too scared to feel angry or indignant or hurt. We were actually able to joke about how screwed up things still were in Bulgaria despite the fact that it had finally joined the European Union in January 2007. He had always wanted to go back home. He was now living full time in Sofia, trying to start his own law firm and working for the Municipality of Sofia. His clients were not paying him, judges still had to be bribed, and the local government was as corrupt as ever. His brother's private firm had been racketeered out of business by predatory tax authorities, and his parents, long retired, still pined for their communist youth and the unfulfilled dream of socialism.

What surprised me most about him was how resigned he had become about it all. My heart was still pounding from the chaos of the morning. The explosion had unnerved me because explosions were things far removed from my daily experience. I had spent most of the last six years of my life in quiet, peaceful Maine, where violence really only existed on television or in video games, where the police were usually the good guys, and where I had never once been asked or expected to pay a bribe to a public official. Whereas I was both scared and outraged about the situation at the airport, Hristo just accepted the reality that was Bulgaria without question. He drank coffee and chatted on his cell phone with Kaloyan.

Hristo had gone back to try to change his country, but his country had changed him. His pessimism was ever present, like an existential cloud that enveloped him. A World Values Survey in 2006 ranked Bulgaria as one of the least happy countries in the world, sharing a category with Moldova, Albania, Iraq, and Zimbabwe. Sitting across from me that late July morning was proof of that statistic. Back at Berkeley I had once known Hristo to be hopeful for the future. He now seemed resigned. I imagined that too much cheating, theft, violence, betrayal, and frustration had robbed him of whatever dreams he had once had. However mad I was at him for other things, I felt sorry for him too.

It seemed that the chaos and violence of the transition had consumed him. It was unfair. It was the first time that I felt how profoundly the collapse of communism in Bulgaria and the nineteen years of the so-called Changes had affected me as well. Before that morning I had never wished so strongly that things in Bulgaria had worked out differently: for the Bulgarians, for him, for us.

CHAPTER 12 **COFFEE**

On his eightieth birthday, she woke up and made him his coffee just the way he liked it: a shot of espresso with two teaspoons of sugar and no milk. He had only one of these each day, savoring each sip with his typical morning breakfast—one hard-boiled egg and a piece of toast with a thick slab of feta cheese on it. If it was summer, she would add fresh tomatoes, otherwise it was just cheese and bread. They had been married for fifty-two years, and he had more or less the same morning meal as long as she could remember. He was a simple man who liked his coffee strong and sweet.

She usually woke up before him, busying herself in the kitchen and wondering about their three grown daughters: two still in Bulgaria, one far off in Sydney. How quickly life had passed them by, how soon their children had grown. It seemed like only moments ago when she was cradling the youngest to her breast while trying desperately to entertain the older two. The harried days and sleepless nights that once seemed like they would never end, how could they be so long gone?

The early mornings in Sofia were always quiet in the hours before the construction workers started on the next ghastly monstrosity of a high-rise in their once exclusive neighborhood. She brushed a strand of her thick gray hair behind her ear and looked down from their seventh-story window onto the streets below.

They were full of potholes now, with German luxury sedans parked haphazardly up on the sidewalks. There were empty beer bottles and discarded plastic bags among the broken benches of the children's playground. It never used to be this way, she thought, turning to the coffee. This had once been a neighborhood for high party cadres, those most committed to building the socialist dream. The conspicuous consumption of the new residents was a thumb in the face of the old *nomenklatura* that still lived here.

She carefully unscrewed the stovetop espresso maker and put two spoonfuls of ground coffee into the small chamber above the water. She thought back. They were both so young when they met: he the son of peasants, she the daughter of a rehabilitated industrialist whose factories had been nationalized after World War II. It was a dangerous thing for him to have married her; her pedigree could have damaged his chances at ever having a respectable career. And she initially disliked his rough manners, being used to a finer life where people spoke in quieter tones. But he had been handsome in his youth, with dark hair and fiery dark eyes. She remembered how good he looked despite the rough workman's clothes he was wearing and the hungry way he had stared at her. She met him at a fruit-canning factory where she worked during the summer after her first year of university. Students were all assigned to summer brigades, doing menial jobs to pay back society for their free higher education. The first thing he had told her was that he was ideologically opposed to her perfume because it was a sign of her bourgeois upbringing. But she knew that he was intoxicated by her scent, a French eau de toilette she had procured through a friend, on the black market. She remembered dabbing it on extra heavy when she knew that he would be overseeing her brigade shift. She would catch him leaning in toward her to inhale her aroma. Men liked the smell of perfume, no matter how bourgeois it was. Even young comrades hoping to become big Communist Party members.

The kitchen floor was cold, so she went out into the hall to put on her slippers. She looked up at the odd assortment of coats and jackets hanging off the hooks and smiled at the memories of bundling up her daughters in the winter as she sent them off to school. The memories warmed her and she hurried back into the kitchen to watch the espresso maker. The trick was not to leave it on the heat too long. The moment the coffee starting spurting out of the narrow tower in the center, it was time to take it off. After fifty years she knew exactly how he liked his coffee.

A young communist work brigade, circa 1950.

He had always been a modest man, even when he had power and influence and status. He never wanted to be special. She loved him because he had made her see the beauty of his dream—that there would be no inequality, that people would come together and build a better future. She smiled to herself remembering his early monologues. How she had laughed at the idea that people were not intrinsically selfish, that it was supposedly the economic system, and not human nature, that made them so. She had raised three children, and she knew that each of her girls had been as self-centered and imperious as the next. How many hours had she spent watching children on the playground, seeing them create scarcity out of abundance for the sake of establishing a hierarchy? She remembered her own daughters always fighting for the green bucket in the sandbox, ignoring the orange and blue ones that were exactly the same. It always had to be the green one. People were just that way, she had always believed, they want the best things for themselves. He had always argued the contrary, but now they both agreed that she was right. There were many days when she was secretly disappointed that his view had been proven wrong. Perhaps human nature could be changed, but she certainly didn't see how.

He had spent decades trying to convince her of his view, and it had been an appealing vision, a dream. It was his passion and his commitment that had most attracted her to him. He so deeply believed in something bigger

Three sisters in the center of Sofia in the 1950s.

than himself, something so noble. What a lovely dream it was, she thought, listening carefully to the espresso maker as it began to gurgle. And he had never given up on that dream, even when the dream began to give up on itself.

She looked at her old Mraz refrigerator. How many times could he have used his privileges to get us a new one, she thought, a nice Gorenje fridge from Yugoslavia? How many times could we have used our connections to get a bigger apartment or some jeans for the girls from the West? But he never let us. Oh, there had been many times when his communist piety had exasperated her—couldn't he have been less stubbornly principled for the sake of his own family? All of the other families were using their positions to improve their situations, but her husband had so adamantly refused.

Even after 1989, when the old rules were wiped away, she had encouraged him to take what he could before the enterprises he directed were sold off to foreign investors. He had refused. She hated him for that then, but in an odd way she loved him for that now. Despite everything, he had remained exactly the same. He refused to become a cynic, to give in to the new rules. He always paid his taxes, always paid the criminally inflated heating and electricity bills, and always bought his tram tickets, even when everyone around him had long decided that the state was too weak to prevent the ubiquitous dishonesty that seized Bulgaria after 1989. "I fought for something right," he would say, "and I won't stop fighting for it just because I am now on the losing side."

She looked down at her hands as she rested them against the edge of the stove. They were wrinkled and dotted with wide brown freckles. I used to have lovely hands, she thought. He used to kiss them and press them against his cheeks. I am just the shell of the woman I used to be, waiting to be useful to my daughters. I am just a remnant of my own existence, a residual of my youth. How beautiful I used to be, and how handsome he was. She closed her eyes and imagined him with his thick, almost black hair, and his broad, strong shoulders. He had a chiseled jaw back then, and firm, full lips. He was just in his twenties when she married him, and she was merely a frightened girl. It was a different time then, she thought, we would not have thought about separating no matter what happened. The girls had always kept them together even when the demands of career and party loyalties threatened to pull them apart. He was her life, and today was his eightieth birthday.

She would have loved to give him back his dreams. She would have loved to give him back the last seventeen years. How much of their savings had they lost when the banks collapsed and were unable to pay out deposits? They were lucky at first because she had always kept some money in cash between the mattresses. But then the hyperinflation ate that up, too. All those years of saving for nothing; all the jewelry he wouldn't let her buy because he wanted to make sure they would have enough for the future. Then he watched his closest friends and colleagues turn into criminals and thieves, hiring wrestlers and body builders to create a culture of fear while they bled state monies into their own Swiss bank accounts. These had been men who once shared his dream, too. And how difficult it had been for him to watch their youngest child, his favorite, move halfway across the world to

A Bulgarian family at the seaside, circa 1980.

Australia, seeking a better future in what she called a "normal" country. She visited only once a year now and only for a week or two. He spent hours in his room looking at her baby pictures every time she left. No, the Changes had not been easy on them; they barely survived on their little pensions. But after fifty-two years they were still together. Surely there was something worthy in that. Not everything had been a failure.

The espresso maker started to sputter, and she turned down the heat. She poured the thick brown liquid into a small cup, a cup that was one of the few remaining of a set she had bought back in 1974 on a vacation in Hungary. They had traveled to Lake Balaton, and he had gotten badly sunburned on his back and could not sleep for two nights. She added the sugar, stirring slowly and wondering if she should change out of her dressing gown before waking him up. It was his birthday after all.

"Good morning," he said from the doorway, rubbing a hand over his still sleepy eyes.

"Good morning," she said, smiling. The dressing gown would have to do.

He was still in his shorts and a worn T-shirt, his once broad shoulders slightly hunched over and his now less defined chin studded with gray stubble. There were deep bags under his brown eyes, and his head was almost completely bare save for a thin semicircle of hair that ran across the

Husband and wife in
the center of Sofia,
circa 1965.

back of his head from one ear to another. The skin of his neck was leathery
and dry, and his lips looked thin and tired.

"Coffee?" she said.

"Mmmm," he said.

He sat down at the small kitchen table in their relatively humble flat. He
had been a deputy minister before 1989, and this was the biggest apartment
the party would allow him. It was tiny compared to the huge flats of his new,
nouveau riche neighbors, but it had been their home for the last forty years.
It was in this kitchen that his wife had gone into labor with their third child.
It was here that he had read his letter of promotion to the Ministry of
Agriculture. It was at this table that his daughters had studied for their
university entrance exams, where he first read the news of his best friend's

The forgotten ones.

defection, where his mother had told him the news of his father's sudden death. He was reading a newspaper in this very room when he first heard about the fall of the Berlin Wall. It was here that he had written his final, exasperated letter of resignation, forcing himself into retirement.

She placed the coffee down on the table and took a seat across from him. He gingerly lifted the cup to his lips, his hands less steady than before. He closed his eyes as he took the first sip.

"Mmm," he said, savoring the liquid on his tongue. It was bitter and sweet at the same time. "Just the way I like it."

She nodded and stretched her hand across the table toward him. She smiled.

He took her hand and squeezed it gently. He lifted it and pressed it to his cheek, gazing into her gold-flecked green eyes. "Just the way I like it."

In April of 2009 Kaloyan and his smart, sociologist girlfriend came to visit me in Maine. I was teaching a course on women and communism and asked if he would be a guest speaker. He was delighted. I showed a short film about his grandfather and then introduced him to the class. My students listened politely for about twenty minutes as he talked about life before 1989.

"We had a normal life," he told them. "I have happy childhood memories like you do. We were not monsters. We were just ordinary people trying to live our lives. Trying to find a way for people to get along together better. Trying to build a better world. We did not succeed, but it was good to have something to try for."

His accent was thick, and I think the students had a hard time understanding his English at first. A few times he looked over at me and asked me to translate a Bulgarian word into English. I don't know what my students had expected him to say, but they seemed thrown off balance. Some of the students raised their hands and asked polite questions, a bit intimidated by him, I think. One of my favorite students finally raised her hand and asked, "Is there anything about communism you would bring back?"

"My childhood," Kaloyan said. I thought maybe he misunderstood the question. But he continued. "I was about eighteen when these Changes happened. Maybe like you, yes? I studied hard in school and did all the things I was supposed to do. But it was for nothing. I wasted my childhood trying to become something in a world that disappeared. The thing I miss about communism is the chance to live the life that I spent my childhood preparing for."

The students nodded politely, not sure what he was really talking about or perhaps just made uncomfortable by the implications of his comments. It could theoretically happen to them too. The class soon ended, and the students rushed off. Kaloyan and I went for a coffee to chat and debrief. It was weird to have him here, a kind of Bulgarian invasion of Maine. We had known each other for over ten years, but we had only ever met in his country. He was having a difficult time in the United States because he could not smoke anywhere. He was desperate to get back home. I asked for our cappuccinos to go, so that he could smoke outside. While we waited, he turned to me and said, "By the way, I finally found one for you."

"One what?"

"A conspiracy theory."

"A good one?" I asked.

"A really good one," he said.

It went something like this. Sometime in the late 1980s the Soviet Politburo came to the realization that they could not economically keep up with the West. The West's vast financial superiority allowed them to outspend the Russians on military technology, and their ability to meet consumer demand was unrivaled. The Soviets had old and outdated factories that produced substandard goods. What they needed was Western technology. For years the KGB had been trying to steal this, but by the late 1980s it became clear that it would be much easier to just ask the West to lend a helping hand. But as long as the Communists were seen as the ideological enemy, there could be no cooperation.

So, according to a secret plan hatched at the very highest level of the Soviet leadership, the USSR would fake its own collapse. They would let the East European countries and certain Soviet republics go their own way, not because they cared about their independence but merely because they had become a financial drag on Russia, the core state of the Soviet Union. An elaborate ruse was planned, and Russian enterprises were to be sold off to foreign investors to bring hard currency and new technology into the country. During this period the Communists would lay low and allow capitalism to work its course, reviving Russia's industrial base but also trampling the well-being of ordinary Russians. According to this theory, once the Russian economy was sufficiently caught up with the West and once the Russian people had had enough of oligarchs and income polarization, the Communist Party would reemerge like a phoenix from the ashes and renationalize all of the previously privatized state-owned enterprises, with the complete support of the Russian people. With this new infusion of technology and capital, the new USSR would be unstoppable.

Marx said that in order to have communism you must pass through the historical stage of capitalism. Bulgaria and Russia tried to go straight from feudalism to communism. This was a mistake. People need to experience the injustice of capitalism to see the value of socialism. Thus, when the time was right, the Communists would be back, protecting the rights of workers, women, the elderly, and the poor, extracting surplus value for the good of the people, trying to build a brighter and more egalitarian future.

When Kaloyan finished telling me this, I raised my eyebrows at him.

"That is a good one."

"I thought you'd like it," he said, smiling.

"But nobody really believes that, do they?"

"Maybe they do. Maybe not." He shrugged. "But it says a lot about what Bulgarians want to believe."

"That communism might come back?"

"That capitalism might someday meet the same fate."

The barista called out, and we walked up to the counter to get our drinks. I grabbed our four-dollar coffees, and we headed outside.

The late afternoon sunshine spilled through the trees, sprinkling little patches of light across the quad. Kaloyan immediately lit up a cigarette. "But let's hope they have the good sense to wait a little while longer," he said, exhaling a lungful of smoke. "I've had enough change for one lifetime."

CHAPTER 14   **TITO TRIVIA**

Where was Tito born? *In Kumrovec.*
Who were his parents? *Franjo and Marija Broz.*
How many older brothers and sisters did he have? *Six.*
What was the name of Tito's paternal great-grandmother?
   Anna Medvedecz.
What was the name of Tito's maternal great-grandfather?
   Andreas Blasichko.
What was the name of Tito's fourth grade teacher? *Stjepan*
   Vimpuhek.

Rada was nine years old in the summer of 1991. She was the
Federal Republican Tito Trivia Champion of Bosnia and Herzego-
vina. After winning a school-wide competition, Rada had pro-
gressed through every level, dazzling the judges with her seemingly endless store of information about the details of Josip Broz
Tito's life, the now deceased leader of the country that was then
called the Socialist Federal Republic of Yugoslavia. As far as Rada
was concerned, Tito was the greatest man who ever lived. She
liked nothing better than to spend her free time studying about his
life. Rada knew everything about him and could answer the judges'
questions as if they were asking her what her favorite color was.

Who was Tito's first wife? *Pelagija Belousova.*
How old was she when she married him? *Fourteen years old.*

How many children did she have? *Five.*

How many survived? *One son.*

The Yugoslav National Tito Trivia Championships were scheduled to be held in Belgrade in the fall. There were only five other champions in Yugoslavia, those five students who had won the republican championships in Yugoslavia's other socialist republics: Serbia, Montenegro, Croatia, Slovenia, and Macedonia. Rada would be competing in the finals to be named the Tito Trivia Champion of all Yugoslavia. It was a title she wanted more than anything else in her young life. She was single-minded in her pursuit of it, the way only bookish nine-year-old girls could be. Rada was rather pretty for her age, slender and graceful with long and curly chocolate-brown hair that reached the middle of her back. Although her eyesight was fine, she wore thick-framed glasses because she thought they made her look more serious. Her parents were both surgeons, spending long hours away from home. Rada's older brother, Goran, was supposed to look after her, but he knew well enough that she would spend her entire afternoons after school reading biographies of Tito's life. He would leave her in the house while he hung out with his friends or spent time fooling around with his new girlfriend, Aisha, in his parents' bedroom. Rada liked Aisha because she did not laugh at Rada's Tito obsession the way so many of Goran's other friends did. Aisha liked Tito too, telling Rada that without Tito there would be no Yugoslavia. Aisha also gave Rada an old portrait of Tito that Aisha's parents had from the early 1960s. Rada told Goran that he should marry Aisha, even though he was only sixteen.

When was Tito awarded the Order of Georgi Dimitrov in Bulgaria?
   September 22, 1965.
When was Tito awarded the Grand Collar of the Order of the
   Andean Eagle in Bolivia? *September 29, 1963.*
When was Tito awarded the Grand Collar of the Order of Almara
   with Sash in Afghanistan? *November 1, 1960.*
When was Tito awarded the Knights Order of the Elephant with
   Sash in Denmark? *October 29, 1974.*
When was Tito awarded the Grand Collar of the Order of the Queen
   of Sheba with Sash in Ethiopia? *July 21, 1954.*
When was Tito awarded the Grand Collar of the Order of Pahlavi
   with Sash in Iran? *June 3, 1966.*

When was Tito awarded the Grand Cordon of the Supreme Order of
the Chrysanthemum in Japan? *April 8, 1968.*

When was Tito awarded the Order of Lenin in the Soviet Union?
June 5, 1972.

Rada spent the entire summer of 1991 sequestered in the library or at home
reading her Tito books and making flashcards with all sorts of facts that she
thought might appear in the competition. She concentrated on dates and
names, making complex chronological timelines of Tito's life. She had a
good memory and knew that she would be able to recall anything that she
put on the timeline. The challenge was to make it as complete as possible.
Of course, there were always holes, questions that were unanswered by the
official history books. What was Tito's shoe size when he died? Did he sleep
on his side or on his back? If on his side, did he prefer the left or right? What
kind of soap did he use? Did he ever suffer from indigestion? Rada knew
these were idle curiosities of hers—the judges would never actually ask
something personal like that. Still, she found herself sometimes daydream-
ing about meeting Tito and asking him all kinds of very personal questions
and then compiling them all into a definitive book of facts about his life.
She would then be the indisputable Tito expert. Of course, she would still
go to university. Rada planned to become a modern historian with a major
in Tito studies. She would be invited to talk shows. She would be able to
travel around the country judging Tito trivia competitions for the rest of her
life—the famous Tito trivia wunderkind who became the Tito Trivia Champion of all Yugoslavia at the age of nine.

In what year did Tito win a silver medal in an army fencing
competition? *1914.*

Where did Tito first meet his Austrian wife, Lucia Bauer? *In the
Hotel Lux in Moscow.*

In what year did Tito open Yugoslavia's borders to all foreigners?
1967.

Where was Tito between the first and fourth of February 1979?
Kuwait.

Rada hardly noticed when Slovenia and Croatia declared their independence on June 25 or when the Croats bowed to European pressure and
agreed to postpone their declaration for three months. Tensions were

mounting all around, and she heard her parents whispering at night in the kitchen, talking about the end of Yugoslavia. Rada knew that there was a lot of talk on TV about politics and nationalism and independence, but she was nine. All of it sounded like grown-up stuff. There was a small war in Slovenia, but it was over quickly. Her mother warned that there could be a bigger war. Rada thought this was just her mother worrying the same way she always worried that Rada would catch cold if she stood too long in a draft. After a while it seemed that Goran and Aisha were also starting to be worried, and this concerned Rada, not because she became aware that her country was falling apart around her but because she did not like to see her brother and his girlfriend so unhappy. She wanted them to marry and have children so she would get to be clever auntie Rada who knew everything about Tito. As the political situation worsened, day-to-day life went on. Rada thought of nothing but the upcoming competition.

How old was Tito when he married Jovanka Broz? *Fifty-eight.*
How old was she? *Twenty-seven.*
Who was the best man at their wedding? *Aleksandar Ranković.*

The Croatian War started in August 1991. Over the next six months, over ten thousand people would be killed, as the republic was ripped apart. Lives were uprooted, homes destroyed, families separated and displaced. There would be no Yugoslavian Tito trivia competition.

When did Tito die? *3:05 p.m., May 4, 1980.*
Where did he die? *In Ljubljana, Slovenia.*
How many kings attended his funeral? *Four.*
How many presidents attended his funeral? *Thirty-one.*
How many prime ministers? *Twenty-two.*

The war would eventually come to Bosnia, too. Sarajevo would be destroyed. Tens of thousands more former Yugoslav citizens would lose their lives. Neighbors would turn on neighbors, friends would betray their friends. Like the Bulgarians, the Yugoslavs would watch their economic system come crumbling down around them. Unlike their eastern neighbor, they would lose their entire country, too. Rada's father would be badly wounded by a shell that hit the hospital. Aisha would be sent to a camp and raped repeatedly by Serbian soldiers. Goran would be drafted into the Bosnian Army and would be killed three days after his nineteenth birthday. Rada and her mother would finally have to flee the house she grew up in, leaving behind all of her books and notes, joining the mass exodus of refugees flooding into the now independent Croatia. Only after the war was over were they reunited with her father. Aisha sought asylum in Sweden. Rada never saw her again.

About seven years after the Dayton Accord, which finally ended the Bosnian War, Rada found herself in the United States, studying at the University of Pittsburgh for a semester. Before returning home to Sarajevo she was given the chance to intern for a young assistant professor at a research center in Washington. Rada took the opportunity. She spent two months in Washington working closely with the American woman who was a newly minted PhD and who knew a fair bit about the Balkans, having lived for over a year in nearby Bulgaria. One night, this woman invited Rada over to her small studio apartment in Rosslyn for dinner. After an evening of easy conversation, they had just opened a second bottle of wine when the American asked about the war. Americans always wanted to know about the war.

Rada took a deep breath, getting ready to deliver her now standard spiel about how grateful the Bosnians were for American support and that without Dayton the war would still be going on. But the American interrupted her before she could start and said, "I am sure you get asked about this all the time. It must be a pain in the ass for you."

"Yes," Rada admitted.

"What I'm curious about is how the war affected ordinary people's lives. I don't care about the politicians or the peacemakers. I care about the individuals. Like you, for instance, what did you lose? What do you regret most about the war?"

Rada thought of Goran. She thought of Aisha. She thought of returning to see her home in Sarajevo completely destroyed. She knew her answer. It was terribly childish, but absolutely true.

"That I never had the chance to become the Tito Trivia Champion of all Yugoslavia."

"What's your favorite lyric?" I asked from the front seat.

"Easy," Elena said from the back. " 'In my dreams I was drowning my sorrows / But my sorrows they learned to swim.' " She switched from Bulgarian to English flawlessly.

"What's yours?" Misho asked me from the driver's seat.

"Oh, I don't know. It depends on my mood. And what country I am in," I said, staring out the window as we waited in line to cross the border into Serbia.

It was August of 2009. I was riding shotgun in a brand new sports utility vehicle with three Bulgarians I barely knew. Hristo had a friend with a spare ticket to the U2 concert in Zagreb and arranged for me to buy that ticket and to hitch a ride with him. It would be close to a nine-hour drive from Bulgaria to Croatia, depending on the time spent at the borders. We would spend two nights there then turn around and drive nine hours back. A Balkan road trip.

My companions were Misho, Elena, and Anastasia. When I met them back at the Starbuck's near the Vasil Levski Stadium in the center of Sofia, the first thing I noticed was that they were all really good-looking. I soon learned that Elena and Anastasia were both actresses. Elena was twenty-five and was just making the transition from stage to film. She had recently won the Bulgarian equivalent of a Tony for best actress. She was tall and thin with porcelain white skin and long brown hair. She had watery, doe eyes and graceful fingers that danced through the air when she talked with her hands. Her perfect white teeth were framed by full, pouty lips, and her smile was sexy and innocent at the same time.

Anastasia was still primarily a stage actress who was also working for a big music promoter in Sofia. At the time she was busy organizing Madonna's upcoming Sticky and Sweet Tour in Bulgaria. She was more voluptuous than Elena and had a more expressive face. Whereas Elena seemed very conscious and deliberate about her beauty, Anastasia was unconcerned and natural. She made funny faces when she talked, allowing her brow to furrow and raising her eyebrows to create a row of horizontal lines across her forehead. She opened her mouth wide when she laughed and sometimes sat crossed-legged on the back seat. She was thirty-three years old and had the kind of personal charisma usually reserved for prophets and dictators. Her hair was also brown, but it was shorter and casually pulled away from her face by a stretchy white headband. She smoked long, skinny cigarettes.

Misho was our driver and the organizer of the excursion. He was thirty-seven, two years younger than I, and was a successful real estate entrepreneur and a member of Bulgaria's emerging upper-middle class. He had been in the music business, managing Bulgarian bands throughout the 1990s and then started his own property management company. He was tall and well built with shaggy reddish-brown hair. He played guitar and oozed the coolness of someone used to hanging around famous people. He was the only one of the three I had met before, and I knew he owned several restaurants around Sofia. We were riding in his new Mitsubishi Jeep. It was the perfect vehicle for a long trip with a top of the line sound system. It also had a refrigerated glove compartment and a talking GPS with a male voice with a British accent whom we affectionately referred to as Charles.

During the first hour or so of our trip, I had not said much. Misho had told Elena and Anastasia that I was American and that I was a professor and a writer and that I spoke Bulgarian. It was clear that they all knew each other, so I let them do most of the talking. It soon became apparent that Elena was a pathological U2 fan. She had prepared a comprehensive playlist on her iPod that would allow us to listen to nine hours of nonstop U2 without repeating the same version of any song twice. She had been in

Berlin just a week earlier to see the U2 concert there and chatted effusively about what a great show it had been, reciting the songs that they had played in order. Despite her playlist, we ended up listening to the new *No Line on the Horizon* album four times in a row as we left Sofia. It was only when they realized that I knew the words to every single song on the new album that I was forced to admit to my own U2 obsession.

"Are you a big U2 fan?" Elena asked.

"This will be my seventh U2 concert," I confessed. "But my first one in Europe."

Misho nodded. He was impressed. "Which tours?"

"Well, I saw them four times for the Joshua Tree tour in 1986 and 1987," I said, and I could see Elena's mouth drop open in surprise. "Once in San Diego, once in LA, and twice in Tempe, Arizona, while they were filming *Rattle and Hum*. I was there for that."

"Oh my god," Elena said. "That is so amazing. I have never met anyone who was there for the making of the movie." She was only three years old in 1987.

"Then I saw them again in 2001 in San Jose for the Elevation tour and for the Vertigo tour in Boston in 2005," I continued.

I had everyone's attention now. "I guess I am a little loopy when it comes to U2," I said.

Elena and Anastasia smiled. It was then that I realized that they had been a little intimidated by my presence because I was an American, I was older, and I was what they considered an "intellectual." When they realized that I was a fellow U2 fan, however, the differences between us were sucked out of the window like the ashes of Anastasia's cigarettes. Once we crossed into Serbia, we spent the next hour talking about music and our favorite songs and our favorite lyrics and sharing all of the varied bits of trivia we knew about the band. Not one of them, not even Elena, could even come close to my encyclopedic knowledge of all things related to Bono and the boys. Before the day was up, Elena would refer to me as her "U2 sister."

Driving with them toward Belgrade, I could not help but think back to my first train ride in the Balkans nineteen years earlier with the ketchup-smuggling Yugoslavs. My initial conversation with them had been about music, too. There was something poetic about being in a car with three Bulgarians now, united with the singular purpose of going to hear the music of a band that we all loved. This was not an ordinary road trip. It was a pilgrimage, a pilgrimage to see the oracle of Dublin. Or at least that is what we decided that we would call it.

Somewhere before Belgrade we stopped for gas, and Anastasia and I bought tall cans of Lasko Pivo, a delicious Serbian lager. One lovely thing about the Balkans is that only the driver is forbidden to drink alcohol; passengers can drink whatever they wish, and all of the gas stations sell beer. The refrigerated glove compartment turned out to be quite convenient.

For some of the time Misho turned the music up and we all sang along to the songs. At other times we sat in silence and let Bono's painful falsetto and the Edge's sweet guitar riffs provide the soundtrack for the breathtaking countryside as it rushed past, dotted with the domes of black-and-white-striped Serbian Orthodox churches.

At the Serbian-Croatian border, the Croatian border guard asked us what the purpose of our visit was. Misho told him that we were going to the u2 concert the following evening.

"The concert has been cancelled," the border guard informed us.

"What?" Misho almost shouted. A wave of panic washed over the jeep. It could not be. We had come so far.

"Bono Vox lost his voice. It will be David Bowie instead."

"Have they rescheduled?"

The border guard laughed a deep hearty laugh. "No, no. Everything is fine."

Misho smiled and took back our passports.

"You scared us."

"Everyone is going to see u2. This will be the biggest rock concert in the history of Croatia," the guard said. "We've never seen so many cars from so many places."

u2 was playing two dates (August 9 and 10) in Maksimir Stadium. It had a capacity of sixty thousand people. Both dates were completely sold out. I was so lucky to have found a ticket.

"The world's best band!" Elena shouted from the back seat.

"Enjoy!" The guard told us as he waved us on.

As we drove toward Zagreb our collective mood turned more conversational. Although we did not know each other that well, being stuck in the cab of a car for hours can induce an incredible amount of familiarity among strangers.

"Do you think people of different nationalities have sex differently?" Anastasia asked.

"You mean like Asians and Africans?" Misho asked.

"No, no. I mean Europeans. Do you think Bulgarians do it differently than Austrians?"

"Greeks do it in the ass!" Misho laughed.

"Turks do it with sheep," Elena added.

"No, I'm serious," Anastasia insisted. "I mean the feeling between a man and a woman, not just the technique. Do people feel differently?"

I didn't mean to say it, but it just came out. "Bulgarians cheat more."

There was a silence in the car. I winced. Anastasia saved me.

"It's probably true. Sex is not such a big deal to Bulgarians."

"Because we get so much of it!" Misho added, trying to change the subject.

"It's not just that," Anastasia said. "I think Bulgarians don't care so much about cheating because we expect that everyone will do it."

"Women too?" I asked.

"Women too."

"I would be angry if my boyfriend cheated on me," Elena said.

"But would you leave him because of it?" Anastasia asked.

Elena thought about it for a long minute. "It depends on the circumstances."

"Bulgarian women can also be really jealous. My ex-girlfriend was always worried that I was cheating on her," Misho added.

Misho explained that he had felt a lot of pressure to get married when he turned thirty-five. It was rare for men in Bulgaria to remain unmarried into their midthirties. He had a serious girlfriend at the time and asked her to move in with him as a trial.

"The minute she moved in she started nagging me all of the time and trying to control me. Women hide their true selves until they think they have you. They are impatient and demanding. I will never get married. I need my freedom."

"Don't you want children?" Elena asked.

"Not really," Misho said. "I want to live comfortably and to do what I want to do without any restrictions. I have enough responsibility in my life without having to worry about a wife and a child."

"Haven't you ever been in love?" Anastasia asked.

"Of course. But it never lasts, and it is bad for business. Business is more important for me than love. Business and music. Which is why I am in the music business."

"Are your parents divorced?" I asked.

"Oh no, they were married until my father died. They were big Communists. My mother still is. She was the director of a library and used to edit the Bulgarian Politburo speeches. I was always in trouble with them. I wanted to be a rock star—you know I play the guitar—so I had to be a rebel. I had to be an anticommunist. Against the system. And I was always working the black market, selling Western cassette tapes and LPs. I got caught twice and almost got kicked out of the Komsomol. My mother used her connections to help me, but I never stopped. I thought it was stupid that we couldn't get Western music. Who the hell was the government to prevent me from listening to Pink Floyd?"

"What does your mother do now?" I asked.

"Well, she is now retired, but she is still very red. She complains about everything. She wants some form of socialism back, I guess. Not the old communism, but something better than we have now. It has not been easy for her."

"Do you have brothers and sisters?"

"I have one sister, and she has two kids. I am the fun uncle."

"What does your mother think of your business?"

"Well, she is happy that I am doing well, but she would have liked me to work at the university. I have a master's degree in history from Sofia University. I wrote my thesis on the Bulgarian Renaissance. She wanted me to study for a PhD, but then the Changes happened. I had all these friends who were musicians, and so I started a music management firm instead."

"Do you want to get married?" I asked Elena, who had been leaning in between the seats to hear our conversation. She seemed to be waiting for an opening so that she could join in and smiled when I finally asked her a question.

"Not yet. I want to have a career first, to express myself artistically."

"Did you always want to be an actress?"

"No, I went to a French-language secondary school, and I was supposed to go to a university in Paris. But then I decided to go to acting school in Bulgaria."

"Did your parents support your decision to become an actress?"

"My grandmother was a professor of literature at Paisy Hilendarski University, and anyone who is anyone in the theater in Plovdiv knew her. Both of my parents are writers. My aunt is a painter. It was only natural that I would also do something creative. Acting was my dream, and my parents wanted me to have my dream come true."

"What about you?" I asked Anastasia, who was listening from the back seat, her cheek against her hand.

"I don't care about being famous," she said. "I am thirty-three, and I don't think I have as much talent as I used to."

"That's not true!" Elena protested.

"Well, I don't care anymore. I just want to fall in love and find a good man. Men in Bulgaria are all so difficult."

"I hear you," I said, smiling at Misho, who shrugged.

"I will soon be thirty-five," Anastasia said. "I am tired of games. I want a normal man. I want to be surrounded by honest people and people who appreciate my honesty. I want to live an honest life. Acting is too much pretending. Sometimes you forget who you are and what you want to be."

"That can happen even when you aren't an actor," I said.

At some point, Misho informed us that we had about an hour to go. He turned up the music when the album *Achtung Baby* came on, and we all sang our way into Zagreb. Charles, the GPS guy, helped us find our way to the hotel, which was an old communist-era complex that had probably been built in the late 1970s. In the twenty minutes it took us to check in, Misho met about five people he knew. A young artist told us that there were supposedly twelve thousand Bulgarians in Zagreb for the concerts. Everyone who was anyone in Bulgaria had come to hear U2.

The next day we all met for breakfast in the hotel. There was not a person in the dining room that did not have on a U2 T-shirt or hat or some symbol of their allegiance. As I was waiting in line for the buffet, I stood behind two Greeks. There were some Germans at a table sitting next to ours, and some Italians sitting behind us. A friend of Misho's from Sofia stopped by our table and told us that he had just met two guys from Beirut who had driven for three days to get to Croatia.

At noon Misho, Elena, Anastasia, and I took a taxi to the center of Zagreb to do some sightseeing and drink some beer before the concert. It was a hot, sunny day, and we craved shade. We went to visit the famous Zagreb Cathedral and poked around in some souvenir shops to buy postcards and presents from Croatia. We had a long, slow lunch in a tourist restaurant across from the cathedral where we traded stories about the places we had traveled to, the books that had touched us, and the things we hoped to accomplish in the next few years. Misho and Elena then discussed the possibility of life after death and reincarnation, with Elena defending the possibility of the latter.

"There are old souls and there are new souls, and it makes a difference which one you are. It affects the kinds of choices you make, although you may not know it. New souls are always cautious. Old souls take more risks."

"I think we just rot," Anastasia stated.

"No," Misho said, "our energy has to go somewhere. It gets recycled somehow, but I don't think that anything of our consciousness is preserved. We only live on in other people. We live on metaphorically."

"Bono is a devout Catholic," I said. "He believes in Heaven."

"Bono is an old soul," Elena interrupted.

"The man has lyrics," Misho added. "They will live on after he is gone."

"He is a prophet," Elena said, her watery eyes twinkling as she brushed her silky hair off of her shoulder. "A prophet of rock and roll."

I laughed at this and felt light. The gospel according to Bono, I thought.

"To the prophet then," Misho said, raising his glass, encouraging us all to drink up before it got too late.

"To the prophet," the rest of us repeated. The beer was cold. For me, nothing is better than an ice-cold beer on a hot summer day. Nothing, that is, except having tickets to a U2 concert.

We took the tram out to the stadium at around 5:00 p.m. We had floor tickets on the ground level, and Misho and I managed to push our way about fifty meters from the front of the stage. Elena met a friend and maneuvered her way right up to the front. Snow Patrol was the first band. They played a long set that was followed by a thirty-minute break. The crowd pushed forward, jostling to get closer to the stage, but no one was letting anyone pass. The stadium was absolutely full.

I was immediately struck by the demographic diversity of the crowd. There were teenagers and people in their late thirties and forties like Misho and me. The other thing was the impressive diversity of nationalities; it was like being in the General Assembly of the United Nations. In the crowd around me, I heard people speaking Croatian, Greek, Bulgarian, Russian, Turkish, Arabic, Italian, English, Spanish, German, Hungarian, Romanian,

The author's precious U2 ticket.

Czech, French, Hebrew, and some Scandinavian language. People had come from all over Europe to Croatia to see this concert. Coming as it did in early August when most Europeans had holidays, they had poured into Zagreb perhaps hoping to combine the show with some beach time on the Dalmatian coast.

More poignantly, there were thousands of Serbs, Croats, and Bosnians in that stadium, three peoples that had brutally slaughtered each other fewer than fifteen years before. Twenty years ago it would not have been possible for sixty thousand Eastern and Western Europeans to come together for a concert. Ten years earlier it would have been impossible for Yugoslav Muslims, Catholics, and Eastern Orthodox Christians to share a peaceful evening of music and celebration. I imagined that this was what Mecca was like for Muslims or Jerusalem for Christians, people laying aside their many differences to worship at the same holy site. But there were no deities in this temple, just four musicians, some instruments, and a lot of fancy lights and video screens.

All at once we heard the music start, and a thunderous roar of elation rose from the stadium. A quartet of rather ordinary looking middle-aged men took the stage, but from the wild jubilation that seized the crowd one could be forgiven for thinking that they were demigods. Screams and shrieks of hysteria burst forth as Bono started to sing. One hundred and twenty thousand hands were simultaneously thrust up toward the sky when he reached out to the crowd. The atmosphere in the stadium was electrified with positive energy as a familiar chorus unified the voices of people once separated by walls and brought together in song those once divided by hatred and war.

For a moment I just listened to the music and the frenzied excitement of the audience, feeling as if I were a part of a congregation in some big, international megachurch. But this was bigger and better than religion because it did not really matter what god you believed in or if you believed in any at all. It was a warm summer night, and the sky was clear. The lights and the guitar and the crowd and the drums and the happiness and the deep, rhythmic bass and the togetherness and the faltering falsetto of one short Irishman seemed to coalesce into an almost transcendent imperative of self-release. Even the otherwise cool Misho was pumping his fists and jumping up and down, his eyes turned up toward the stage where Bono crooned and writhed just fifty meters in front of us. It was like being seventeen years old in Tempe all over again, before I had ever stepped foot in Eastern Europe, before the fall of the wall. But it was 2009, and I was thirty-nine. I was a grown-up now, who had been married and divorced, who had a seven-year-old daughter and a real life. Even though things were far from perfect, I was truly glad that the world had not ended like I had once been so sure that it would.

My heart lifted like a balloon, and tears of happiness spilled onto my cheeks. I threw my head back as the band segued into their second song. I just stood still for a moment and let the music wash over me.

"Are you okay?" Misho shouted into my ear.

"Never better," I said, throwing my arms up. I took a deep breath and started shouting along to the songs, one voice in a chorus of sixty thousand. They were just rock songs, but for those two hours they were the psychic threads that bound us all together into one swaying mass of humanity.

The concert was like a drug, and we filtered out of the stadium high on adrenaline and rock and roll. Misho and I met up with Elena and Anastasia and strolled for an hour or so through the streets of Zagreb from the stadium to the center of town. We all walked arm in arm, and Elena snapped pictures of us as we sang songs and relived the best moments of the concert. We had all shared something incredible, and we wanted to commit every detail of it to memory. I felt like these three Bulgarians were my best friends even though I had only met them one day before.

When we got to the center of town it was well past midnight. We found a little bar where we could buy beers. We sat outside in the warm air, and I joined Anastasia and Misho in a celebratory cigarette. Elena ordered tea and made me write her a message on the inside of the tea bag wrapper. Apparently she had a collection of these from people all over the world. Misho and Anastasia had already done it for her. I don't remember exactly what I wrote, but I signed it "your U2 sister."

We talked a long time about the concert, about how it made each of us feel, and about the joy that music can bring. After a while the conversation turned to Bono's political activism and eventually to politics. Anastasia asked me about how Americans felt about the election of Barack Obama, who had been inaugurated just eight months earlier.

"Well, speaking for myself, I am thrilled. I hated Bush."

"Bush was a cretin," Misho offered.

"Yes," I said, "I was proud of my country for electing Obama. It shows that things can change."

"Do you really think things can change?" Anastasia asked.

"Yes, I think so. And certainly young people like my students, you know, kids in their late teens and early twenties, they got energized by this election. Obama gave us hope."

"It's only temporary," Misho said. "Politicians are all the same."

"No, I don't think so. I believe that Obama will be different. That this won't just be the same."

"Do Americans have hope? Real hope that things will get better? Even after the crisis?" Anastasia asked in a serious tone. It was already past 2:00 a.m. It seemed late for the conversation to turn philosophical. But I liked Anastasia immensely, and I knew she would take offense if I blew off her question, no matter how late it was.

"I hate to make national generalizations, but I do think Americans are a little naïve sometimes," I said. "The French call us the 'big children,' and I think there is something to that. We are always willing to give things a second chance. We are always willing to hope, even when we have been proven wrong."

"Maybe it is naïve, but it is probably better. Bulgarians have no hope. We lost the ability to hope. Anyone who tells you that things will get better is a politician and a liar."

I looked to Elena and Misho and they nodded in agreement.

"Politics is for criminals," Misho said.

"But in a democracy the people choose the politicians."

The cover of a membership book for the Georgi Dimitrov Communist Youth Organization.

"There is no real democracy," Misho spat, lighting up another cigarette. "Everyone knows that elections are bought and sold. You have to have money to have power."

"It's true," Elena said.

"We are just bitter," Anastasia said. "Bulgarians like me are tired. We are a generation betrayed. The Communists told us things would get better and we believed them. But they got worse, and then they ran off with all of our money. Then democracy came along and our leaders told us that things would get better. And we believed them, too. But nothing changed, and they stole our money, too. I have spent my whole life waiting for things to get better, waiting for a future that was promised to me, but that never appears."

Anastasia offered me another cigarette and I took it. I studied my companions one by one. Elena was reclining back in her chair, her arms gracefully draped at her sides. Misho had his elbows on the table and looked intently at Anastasia who leaned to the right because she had her legs crossed. The three of them represented the last generation of Bulgarians whose lives had been bifurcated by the Changes. Elena had been a mere five-year-old, but Anastasia had been thirteen and Misho had been seventeen when the Changes occurred. They had lived almost half their lives under one system before another replaced it.

"You know I went to school in the center of Sofia when the Changes happened," Anastasia said. "I remember the day they took the red star from the top of the Party House."

The Party House was the former headquarters of the Bulgarian Communist Party. It was part of a cluster of buildings in the center of Sofia built in the 1950s in the style of socialist classicism. The Party House was topped by a tall spire, and atop the spire was a large red star. It was the symbol of communism, and it had shone over the center of Sofia for over forty years.

"We heard the helicopter come," Anastasia continued, "it was the year that I was supposed to join the Komsomol. I was going to be a party member, I believed in communism. I was with some friends and we watched them hook up the star to the helicopter. We couldn't believe what they were doing. It took them a long time, and we thought they would give up. But then they did it. They flew off with the star."

Anastasia's voice was filled with disbelief. I thought about the movie *Goodbye, Lenin* and wondered how many other Bulgarians had seen the star come down. I imagined how I would feel if I saw some huge helicopter fly off with the Statue of Liberty or watched the dismantling of the Lincoln Memorial. This was the stuff of science fiction for me. For Anastasia it was real.

"You know I was supposed to join the Komsomol," she repeated. "I had my life planned out. I remember wondering what was going to happen to me, what was going to happen to my parents and my friends. Everything was so confusing. Those first few years were so hard."

"It was confusing," Misho said, "But it was for the best. We are part of Europe now. We can travel freely and listen to whatever music we like."

"I suppose," Anastasia said, hesitating. "Yes, I suppose we have more opportunities now, and I am not a Communist or anything. But sometimes I think we have too many opportunities, too many choices, choices that don't really matter, choices that exist to make us spend more money, and not choices that help us to be happier people. I think about it a lot these days. I

The Council of Ministers building in the center of Sofia. The red star of communism used to sit atop the spire where the Bulgarian flag now flies.

wonder if I would have been a happier woman under communism, even if I did have fewer choices. Maybe too many choices makes us unhappy. I certainly would have worried less about whether I was making the right ones."

"But can you imagine being stuck in your own country like a prisoner?" Misho asked. "Not being able to say what you like or to express yourself artistically." He looked to Elena who shrugged.

"I don't remember much about communism," she said, "But my parents certainly think they lived better before the Changes."

"Even with the censors and secret police?" Misho asked.

"They don't talk much about that," Elena said.

"My mom thinks the same way," Misho admitted, "she believes it was better before."

"I don't know," Anastasia sighed. "I don't know what to believe in any-

A piece of graffiti from the center of Sofia in June 2010. It reads, "Liberty. Equality. Fraternity." It is accompanied by an image of the red star and a hammer and sickle. Someone else has put a black line through it.

more because I think everything is a lie. I don't want to be rich, and I don't want to be famous. I just want a steady job and good family and a quiet, normal life. Why does that have to be so hard?"

The question hung in the air with the cigarette smoke. A few moments of silence passed. Elena yawned. Misho asked us if we wanted more beers or if we should head back up to the hotel. It was late and the narcotic effects of the concert were finally starting to wear off.

It was 3:07 a.m. when we found a taxi to take us back to the hotel, and we chatted only briefly about the plan for tomorrow. It would be a very long drive back to Sofia, and Misho wanted to get an early start. Misho had business in Sofia the day after, and I would be heading back to the United States in less than a week. We all hugged and kissed each other goodnight.

The pilgrimage was over. We had seen what we had come to see. And like those other pilgrims in Chaucer's *Canterbury Tales*, we learned that a pilgrimage is not only about getting to your final destination. It's about hearing the stories of your fellow travelers along the way.

LOST IN TRANSITION, 2010

In the fall of 2009, just a few months after the U2 concert in Zagreb, my phone started ringing and a few perplexed colleagues asked me, "What the hell is going on with Bulgaria?" The question was prompted by a new study that had just been released to coincide with the twentieth anniversary of the fall of the Berlin Wall. The US-based Pew Research Center's Global Attitudes Project conducted a public opinion survey in nine postcommunist countries to investigate how public attitudes had changed in the twenty years since the historic events of 1989. The survey found widespread disenchantment with the coming of democracy and free markets to Eastern Europe. In Poland, the Czech Republic, Ukraine, Russia, Slovakia, Bulgaria, and Hungary, a nationally representative sample of respondents were asked, "how much have ordinary people benefited from the changes since 1989/ 1991—a great deal, a fair amount, not too much, or not at all?"[1] In all but the Czech Republic, less than half of the population responded with "a great deal" or "a fair amount," with the numbers being the most striking in Bulgaria and Ukraine. In Bulgaria only 11 percent of respondents claimed that ordinary people were better off by a "great deal" or a "fair amount" since 1989, and only 10 percent of Ukrainians and 21 percent of Russians believed that the changes had benefited ordinary people a "great deal" or a "fair amount" since 1991.[2] The survey also found that the number of

Bulgarians who approved of the change to democracy had decreased from 76 percent in 1991 to 52 percent in 2009; 62 percent of Bulgarians said that they were economically worse off today than they were under communism with an additional 18 percent saying that their situation is about the same as it was before 1989.[3] Only 13 percent of Bulgarians felt that they were better off in 2009 than they were under communism. Furthermore, 76 percent of Bulgarians said they are unsatisfied with how democracy is working in their country.[4] Overall, the survey found a growing sense of nostalgia for the communist past, with ordinary men and women increasingly willing to trade in democratic freedoms for economic prosperity.

When the Pew Research Center released this data, I found myself needing to explain the roots of the disenchantment in Bulgaria. Of course Bulgaria exhibited an extreme case of frustration with the Changes, but the survey clearly showed that this frustration was appearing in all of the postsocialist countries, and some feared that the dire numbers for Bulgaria were prescient of an emerging trend in the region. Many of my students and colleagues expressed incredulity at this growing nostalgia, perplexed that East Europeans would collectively long for what was a totalitarian system of government, complete with one-party rule and an oppressive police apparatus that brooked no dissent. More importantly, my colleagues in political science worried that this growing nostalgia would have contemporary political consequences. Other strongmen rulers like Vladimir Putin in Russia might easily capture the imagination of electorates fed up with the chaos and corruption that accompanied the democratic reforms of the last two decades. It is therefore essential that we understand the legacies of twentieth-century communism, not least because they still have very real impacts on the world today.

I offer some scholarly reflections and thoughts about the twenty years that have passed since the fall of the Berlin Wall and the final collapse of the Soviet Union, using the Bulgarian case study as an example that can shed light on the rest of the postsocialist world. Although I know that this may seem like an unwelcome departure from the narrative lightness of the rest of the book, I believe it is important to pull some of the threads together into a brief conclusion.

The nostalgia for totalitarianism is prima facie puzzling to many in the West, particularly if it includes some real tendency toward bringing back any sort of political system that entails one-party rule. Some might be inclined to dismiss it as a momentary cultural trend, but this would be ignoring the fact that the nostalgia has not dissipated in the last twenty years and appears to be growing stronger. For example, in November of 2010, Boiko Borisov, the democratically elected prime minister of Bulgaria, caused a political uproar by publically praising the country's communist dictator: "It would be a tremendous success for any government to build one percent of what [Todor Zhivkov] has built for Bulgaria . . . and achieve the economic growth of the state at that time." Borisov said, "The fact that 20 years after Zhivkov's fall from power nobody has forgotten him shows that many things have been accomplished. It is also a fact that for 20 years now we have been just privatizing what had been built during his time."[5] It was the first time that an elected official gave such a positive assessment of Bulgaria's communist past, giving voice to the sentiments of many ordinary Bulgarians. Borisov's televised comments shocked many observers both inside and outside of the country and provided evidence that sympathy for the communist past may prove increasingly popular with democratic electorates.

If we want to understand what is happening in places like Bulgaria (and perhaps especially in Russia and Ukraine), we need to understand where this nostalgia comes from. From where does the cynicism toward democracy and capitalism arise, and how can it be that people really feel that their lives are worse off today than they were before 1989 when there were travel restrictions, consumer shortages, and secret police? It is here that the study of everyday life can be most useful. No matter how oppressive the political system was, it is always important to recall that life went on under communism. The quotidian aspects of life were unavoidably shaped by the nature of these regimes, but everyday activities often seem to operate independently of politics. People fell in love, had families, and made coffee in the morning against the background of totalitarianism, but it was the coffee making and the falling in love that always took precedence in their lives. They lived these lives in a society where there was relative economic security and order and had come to take these things for granted. Furthermore, communist governments justified their rule by appealing to noble goals, and the rhetoric of equality and justice allowed many people to ignore the most negative aspects of the regime. Finally, the transition to capitalism was handled in a disastrous way, disorienting people and upsetting the daily rhythm of life. The things that they took for granted suddenly disappeared, and they collectively came to reassess the value of their old system just as they were faced with the task of renegotiating the unfamiliar terrain of a new one.

Indeed, countless studies since the early 1990s have shown that Bulgarians long for the security and order of communism. There were, of course, always going to be people like Damiana, who lost the love of her life because of the Bulgarian secret police, but there were many more people who found love and started families before 1989. The problem is that in the West we only tend to hear about the Damianas, because their experiences make better stories and fit more easily into our preconceived notion of what life under communism was like. Witness, for instance, the success of the German film *The Lives of Others*, a tragic love story about a writer and his actress lover who were under relentless surveillance by the East German Stasi. But what about all of the other people, the ones nobody makes films about, those who just got on with their lives? They are the silent majority that we are inclined to forget. Nothing especially tragic or interesting happened to them, so their stories seldom get told.

It is this population of people that suddenly shows up in the national public opinion polls. Although one always has to look critically at the quantitative data, it can sometimes be useful in outlining broader patterns. I will present some of these numbers here to show how Bulgaria fits in among the other former Eastern Bloc countries. Over the past decade, there have been a wide variety of national surveys that show that this nostalgia for the communist past is growing more pervasive. Using the New Europe Barometer of 2001, two Swedish political scientists found increasing nostalgia for the material security of communism across Eastern Europe with a majority of postcommunist citizens evaluating the command economic system in positive terms, even if it meant that they could not always get the bottle of perfume that they wanted.[6] Moreover, throughout the region the polls showed that the percentage of people who approved of a return to communism increased substantially between 1993 and 2001, with an average of 22 percent of the population in seven East European countries desirous of a return to totalitarian Communist rule.[7] These political scientists argued that the desire for a return to the previous system was symptomatic of a "dissatisfaction with the present system's ability to deliver the goods—material or non-material," meaning that not only did people feel materially more poor, but ideologically poor as well.[8]

In Russia, nostalgia for the Soviet period also remains strong. In 2001, 57 percent of Russians said they wanted a return of the USSR, and 45 percent claimed that communism was better than the current system of democracy.[9] In 2009, 58 percent of Russians agreed (30 percent "completely" and 28 percent "mostly") that it is a great misfortune that the Soviet Union no longer exists, although this number may reflect the loss of empire and superpower status as much as it reflects the loss of the communist economic system.[10] A 2007 survey of over a thousand Germans by the Forsa Institute found that only 3 percent of those from the east claimed that they were "very satisfied" with the way democracy was working in the reunified Germany. Furthermore, the same survey found that 73 percent of Germans from the east felt that "socialism was a good idea in principle, but had been poorly implemented" and more than 90 percent believed that they had better social protections before 1989.[11] A 2008 survey of a thousand Hungarians found that the majority believed that life had been better in the years immediately preceding the collapse of communism, and 60 percent felt that the years since 1989 have been the most miserable of their lives.[12]

Citizens of postsocialist states also perceived a large gap between the abstract principles of democracy and the political systems under which they currently lived.[13] In the eight postsocialist states that the Pew Research Center surveyed in 2009 (excluding only East Germany), a majority of respondents agreed that a "strong economy" is more important than a "good democracy."[14] East Europeans were also somewhat more likely to answer that it is more important "that the state play an active role in society so as to guarantee that nobody is in need" than "that everyone be free to pursue their life's goals without interference from the state," with responses in favor of needs over individualism ranging from 51 percent in the Czech Republic to 72 percent in Bulgaria.[15] This means that in Bulgaria less than a quarter of the population preferred individual freedom from state interference over state intervention to prevent need (in contrast, in the United States 55 percent of respondents favored freedom over 36 percent who preferred state intervention to prevent need).

Admittedly, this nostalgia is more pronounced among the older generations.[16] In all societies the elderly often feel nostalgic for the period of their youth. It is no surprise that older men and women like Misho's mother or the fictional elderly couple in "Coffee" would pine for the socialist past, since it was the time when they were young. But it is another matter altogether when young people like Ani, the Bulgarian Turkish woman, says she misses the word *comrade* or when Anastasia decides that fewer choices in life would make her a happier person. There is also quantitative evidence that young people are nostalgic for the communist past, even those born after its demise. This is a bigger puzzle and begs for a more nuanced explanation.[17]

One key to understanding the persistence of nostalgia is to understand the power and enduring nature of the Marxist critique of capitalism. Although I do not have the space to go into any details here, it is important to realize that much of the original communist critique is still valid today and can help explain the volatile nature of free markets. Moreover, those who were born and raised under communism (or who had parents who were born and raised under communism) were equipped with a theoretical model that both predicted and exposed the flaws inherent in the capitalist economic model. A critical factor in the Communists' success in the twentieth century was their tireless criticism of the many real injustices associated with the capitalist system that emerged after the Industrial Revolution (that is, imperialism, colonialism, militarism, poverty, inequality, and so on). The United States supported brutal dictators like Augusto Pinochet in Chile or unjust systems like apartheid in South Africa in order to protect private property and prevent socialism, even if the socialist leaders could take power through free and fair democratic elections. Marxism-Leninism claimed that it could create a more just economic system in a utilitarian sense: that the sum total of happiness in a society would be greater when the interests of the many took precedence over the interests of the few. Like the eighty-year-old husband in "Coffee," there were people who truly believed that the communist system would be a better one. It is these people who have been the most critical of the chaos and economic contractions that followed 1989, and after the beginning of the current global financial crisis in 2008 they have found a growing audience for ideas that had more or less been discarded for two decades.

Moreover, despite its own flaws, it is essential to recall that the command economic system worked well for a while. A state-directed economy had some tremendous advantages for ordinary people who could be guaranteed full employment and have all of their basic needs met. Countries like Bulgaria, Romania, and Yugoslavia went from being peasant backwaters to newly industrialized societies in league with a world superpower. The

USSR created a trading bloc that allowed poor countries to access natural resources and industrial goods that would otherwise have been beyond their means. The standard of living for workers rose rapidly, as did literacy rates and life expectancy. Across the world new nations emerging from Western colonial subjugation turned to the Soviets for resources and assistance. At the same time the Soviet Union managed to train enough scientists to keep up with the West technologically and provided a real resistance to Western political and economic hegemony. It looked for a while that Khrushchev might make good on his promise to bury capitalism.

For a wide variety of reasons that are still greatly contested by scholars, and which are too varied and complex to go into detail here, the system began to falter by the 1980s. Many of the centrally planned enterprises were operating at loss, and guaranteed full employment combined with a system that met all basic needs provided few incentives for worker productivity. People could not be fired and did not need to work to eat or send their children to school. Furthermore, whereas previous generations had believed in the ideological goals of the workers' state, young people lost touch with the original justification for the command economy. Early generations were told that the centralized state was a temporary measure to collectivize property and to resist Western opposition. In Marxist theory the state was supposed to wither away eventually; true communism was a stateless society. But Communist governments showed little desire to dismantle themselves and instead recreated hierarchies of privilege that exposed the hypocrisy of what was supposed to be an egalitarian society. The system also failed to produce the correct amount of the goods and services that people actually wanted, leading to consumer shortages that were ultimately rectified by Western imports. Some countries took hard currency loans from the West to pay for Western goods and became mired in debt, and it was the amount of external debt that would factor greatly in how a country made the transition from a centrally planned to a free-market economy.[18] It is the process of transition and the poor way it was handled in many countries that lies at the root of the growing nostalgia.

Postsocialist countries differed in how state-owned assets were transferred to private ownership after 1989, a process that was called privatization. In some countries, such as the Czech Republic, public assets were privatized by issuing vouchers to each citizen for their share of what had technically been the collectively owned means of production. These vouchers could be sold or traded on the stock exchange, but in principle they were recognition of the idea that communism had been a so-called workers' state and that the workers were in fact the true owners of the country's assets. The government had only been the caretaker of the collectively owned wealth of the nation; it belonged to the people and should be returned to them.

Bulgaria was one of the countries that emerged from the immediate postsocialist period with debt to the West, creditors who demanded to be paid in hard currency. When the Soviet economic trading bloc collapsed, Bulgaria had no markets upon which to sell its industrial goods. Without export markets, and without financial aid from the USSR, Bulgaria had to raise the money some other way. Although an early post-1990 government toyed with the idea of repudiating the loans altogether, diplomatic pressures made this a near impossibility. As the economy continued to falter and political instability increased (because of CIA interference, if we are to believe the theories of Kaloyan and Hristo) it was only a matter of time before Bulgaria's state-owned enterprises would be sold to private investors in order to raise the cash necessary to service the state's foreign debts. This meant that the Bulgarian workers would not be getting their fair share of the supposedly collectively owned assets of the nation.

The privatization process was contested and chaotic, and in the end the wealth of the nation was transferred to a few well-connected foreigners and a new local class of oligarchs and criminals. They used the uncertainty created by the transition process to transform formerly state-owned assets into their own private property through deceit, graft, corruption, intimidation, and violence. Ordinary people inevitably felt that they had been robbed by the privatization process. Communist ideologues had warned that capitalism was an immoral system, and privatization seemed to provide empirical evidence that those who were the least scrupulous were the ones that benefited the most from the sudden dismantling of the socialist system. My art historian friend Dimitar in "New Carpets for Old Kilims" said that there would always be rewards for being an "asshole." Nowhere was this more true than in the countries emerging from communism.

For example, most privatization contracts, which legally transferred state assets to private owners, stipulated that current employees had to be retained and that the privatized enterprise would continue to operate for a minimum of two years. For most enterprises, however, the sale price was often lower than the total sum of the parts if they were broken up and sold for scrap. In the case of previously state-owned hotels, for example, foreign investors could make more money selling the furniture, windows, plumbing, and toilet fixtures than they could in actually trying to run the private business. The privatization contracts were supposed to prevent this and to protect the rights of workers employed in these enterprises while they searched for work on the newly competitive labor markets. The idea was to make the transition gradual.

In reality there was little that could be done if the new owners went ahead and scrapped the enterprises for parts anyway. The political instability of postsocialist governments meant that there were few enforcement mechanisms and there was no threat of renationalization if the investor abrogated the terms of the contract. Even if the government was able to intervene, by the time the enterprises were renationalized all of their valuable assets would have been sold off and the money spirited away into the bank accounts of non-Bulgarians. This process happened for hundreds of enterprises, which were bought and intentionally run into bankruptcy so that their assets could be sold off in a fire sale.[19] The ideological justification for this was that markets were always more efficient than states. If the government had just scrapped the enterprises on its own, however, the money earned could have been used to pay the country's external debts, while also supporting its faltering social safety net to ease the worst effects of the transition for those workers put out of work by the privatizations. Instead, the state was simply bled dry, Bulgarian industry was crushed, and a new class of mafia elites took over the country.

For some young people, like my art historian friend Dimitar, my U2 brother Misho, or the conspiracy aficionado Kaloyan, capitalism brought with it a host of new opportunities for individual success. For others, like Hristo, the fictional Yordanka who sold her hair to pay for her father's medicine, or the fictional Petar who got cheated by the taxi driver, life in Bulgaria became a series of one injustice after another. The new opportunities combined with the new hardships left most Bulgarians confused. They did not know what to think of this process or understand the new rules of the game. A popular joke ran that "everything the Communists told us about communism was wrong, but everything they told us about capitalism was right," meaning that the communist assessment of capitalism as a corrupt and immoral system was correct. The disastrous consequences of unbridled and unregulated free markets were believed to be the product of a sham democracy, where the rich created different brands of political parties to dupe the people into accepting oligarchy.

As a result of all of this, it should be no surprise that more and more people are resurrecting the old Marxist-Leninist critiques of capitalism and reconsidering the so-called efficiency of the free market. For example, Bulgaria's populist prime minister, Boiko Borisov, announced in April 2010 that he was seriously considering the renationalization of previously privatized electric utilities. The three distribution companies, owned by Czech, Austrian, and German foreign investors, bought electricity from the state-owned nuclear power plant and resold it to Bulgarian consumers at more than double the price. Borisov implicated political lobbyists and corrupt privatization contracts in the "robbery" of the Bulgarian people.[20] In May 2010 the Bulgarian nationalist party Ataka proposed new state regulations that would impose caps on the interest rates that banks could charge for consumer loans, leading some economically liberal politicians to argue that the nationalists want a return to communism.[21] Indeed, it often seems that any attempt at state regulation of private enterprise, even regulation that would be considered quite normal in the West, is taken as evidence of a return to totalitarianism, even if this is regulation that would protect the very consumers, workers, and citizens that voted the government into power. It is therefore no wonder that people would long for their totalitarian past, since the current rhetoric in many postsocialist states (and capitalist ones, too!) is that only "totalitarian" governments regulate private enterprises.

When studying the postsocialist era, I often remember the taxi driver I quoted in the introduction: he told me that when you are building a new house, you live in the old one until the new one is ready. An old decrepit house is always better than no house at all and much better than homelessness with the promise of a better house at some undetermined point in the future. Yes, the police state that prevented Damiana from meeting her lover in Cuba was not a good thing, but the corrupt state that followed, with no ability to enforce the laws, was really not much better. You should not disband the army until peace is secured. Otherwise, you will have social chaos.

Although different socialist countries admittedly made the transition in different ways, they all rushed headlong into the free market without taking full stock of the human costs of the Changes, costs that would inevitably come back to haunt them. The moral foundations of society were ripped apart, disorienting ordinary people who did not understand the internal logics of the system. I often think about the peasants who traded their kilims for the cheap new carpets. How were they to even know that it was a scam? If someone came to my house and offered me a hundred dollars for an old rug I would immediately be suspicious of their intentions, because I grew up with the understanding that it is expected that people in a capitalist system should be on the lookout for those who are trying to scam them. It is normal; our lives in the United States are full of potential scams, and we have learned to guard against them. We tell our children, "if it seems too good to be true, it probably is" and "there is no such thing as a free lunch." We know to expect that used car salesmen and insurance adjusters are out to screw us, and that we are constantly being convinced to buy things we really don't need. But postsocialist citizens were largely unaware of how things worked in a capitalist society. Many Bulgarians I met believed that "democracy" meant that they would have the consumer goods of capitalism combined with the social safety nets of socialism. Instead, many of them got neither. They lost their jobs while gaining the right to vote.

This loss of employment created new conditions of poverty at precisely the moment when the social supports were disappearing. Even though there were examples of well-functioning social democracies in Western Europe (that is, the Scandinavian countries), the reigning orthodoxy of Western democratic advisors in Eastern Europe after 1989 was that the communist state had to be totally dismantled.[22] The baby would be thrown out with the bathwater. Twentieth-century communism had to be destroyed completely lest there be any chance of its resurrection. Everything associated with it, even humble attempts at market regulation, were automatically associated with totalitarianism. There could be nothing good about communism. This is the ideological legacy that has been inherited today, and it is a legacy that is increasingly being called into question by ordinary people like Ani, Anastasia, Kaloyan, Hristo, and millions of other men and women throughout the former socialist bloc.

The communist experiment was driven by good intentions, with the idea of creating a more just society that would alleviate some of the most egregious injustices of the market system. These were ideological goals that many people believed in and lived their lives by, no matter how corrupted these goals ultimately became in practice. There *were* good things about the socialist system even if the whole thing was a failure in the end. Writing for the British newspaper the *Guardian* on November 9, 2009, the twentieth anniversary of the fall of the Berlin Wall, the Bulgarian historian Maria Todorova reflected:

> Lamenting the losses that came with the collapse of state socialism does not imply wishing it back. Not all aspects are missed. Mainstream ideological treatment, however, would like us to believe that it was all one package, that one cannot have full employment without shortages, inter-ethnic peace without forced homogenization, or free healthcare without totalitarianism. . . . Post-communist nostalgia is not only the longing for security, stability and prosperity but also the feeling of loss for a specific form of sociability.[23]

Todorova reminds us that it is erroneous to equate social solidarity and economic security with totalitarianism. More significantly, she emphasizes the experiences of ordinary people and what was lost in the lives of individual men and women when socialism fell: work, education, health care, and a feeling of community. Of course people would miss things like this.

People had ordinary lives under the communist system. It was a world just like ours is, with its daily routines and stresses and frustrations and triumphs. After I had my daughter, I remember reading Natalya Baranskaya's novella *A Week Like Any Other*.[24] This Russian novella is about a woman in the Soviet Union trying desperately to combine her job as a scientist with her role as a mother of two young children, never having enough hours in any given day to get everything done. I was stunned to realize how similar my life in the first decade of the twenty-first century was to hers in the 1960s; we were both working mothers trying to balance the challenges of child rearing and career building while maintaining some semblance of sanity. It did not matter that we lived under two completely opposite political and economic systems; the rhythm of our daily lives was structured by the same forces of the quotidian, of getting kids to school, grocery shopping, trying to succeed at work, trying to find time to sleep, and so on. The overall structures within which we completed these tasks were different, but the tasks themselves were remarkably the same. And then one day her world was gone.

We all have our daily routines, waking up in the morning and making coffee, meeting with friends, spending time with our families, or going to work or to school. For most of us these routines are the things that consume our days and structure our time; the political and economic system within which we live is just a backdrop. What do I care about campaign finance reform or banking regulations when I am worrying about getting that stack of papers graded in time so that I can attend my daughter's school play? Although we don't often think about it, the system is always there, and the system is what historically defines us as citizens of particular countries. Think of all the hundreds of thousands of people who lived in ancient Rome; we know almost nothing about that vast majority of them except that they lived at that time under that particular empire. We can only guess what their lives were like by trying to understand the political and economic system under which they lived. But as we are in the process of living our lives, we seldom pay attention to these larger structures. That is, unless they suddenly go away.

Misho and Hristo and the young men on the train with me from Istanbul to Belgrade had all been raised with a package of skills and attitudes that would allow them to be successful under the old system. Ani had been taught that the word *drugar* (comrade) was a sign of desirable equality and respect between teachers and students, and Rada believed that Tito was a national hero. Anastasia watched the red star of communism flown away just before she was going to join the youth arm of the Communist Party; Kaloyan mourns the childhood he spent preparing for a life he never got the chance to live. Everyone had to shift course midstream. It may not have been the best system around, it may even have been a horribly oppressive one, but it was the system that shaped and defined their ideals, attitudes, and life possibilities. Its disappearance was bound to be felt as a loss.

All societies have their pros and cons, and there are always going to be trade-offs that benefit some at the expense of others. It is essential to respect the internal logics that make any particular set of trade-offs seem reasonable within a specific society. We should also pay attention to what we are giving up in exchange for the things that we think we value and how we have learned to value those things in the first place. We pass these values on to the next generation, and they inherit both our dreams and disappointments. Young people, like Elena in "Pilgrims from Sofia to Zagreb," who never really lived under communism, can feel this nostalgia and are left wondering if there could have been a better way, if things might have been different.

I remember an evening back in 2003 when I was sitting in the apartment of my in-laws working on my computer and watching an old communist-era Bulgarian movie on TV. My then fifteen-year-old nephew walked into the sitting room to briefly join me before heading out to be with his teenage buddies. I had first met the son of Hristo's brother when he was a seven- or eight-year-old living in the United States with his parents. I could not believe how big he'd grown in the last few years, suddenly turning into a young man. There was actually hair starting to appear on his upper lip, and it would perhaps be only months before the little, cheerful boy I remembered would have to start shaving. He flopped on the couch next to me with a bag of paprika-flavored potato chips and gazed absentmindedly at the TV.

"Whatcha watching?" he asked.

"Some old Bulgarian movie," I said, half absorbed in my e-mail.

My nephew stared at the TV set as the protagonist hurried through the streets of downtown Sofia. The movie was set sometime in the late 1970s or early 1980s.

"Is that Sofia?" he asked me.

"Of course," I said, "don't you recognize Tsar Osvoboditel Boulevard?"

"Yeah," he said, clearly puzzled. "It is just that I've never seen Sofia that clean. Looks like a totally different city. I never knew that Sofia was ever so clean."

I looked back to the TV. It was true; the center of Sofia actually looked quite beautiful in the film. There was no trash in the streets, no stray dogs, and no graffiti. I looked at my nephew; he was born in 1988. He would have absolutely no memories of what things were like in Bulgaria under communism, neither the good things nor the bad things. He was part of a new generation of Bulgarians, raised after the Changes, and like it was for my students in Maine, communism and the Cold War were ancient history to him. Or were they?

I watched him as he stared at the TV screen, the disbelief apparent on his face. I imagined what he was thinking: that Bulgaria had been a much cleaner place before the transition. No matter what they taught him in school, what the official history books said, or how many communist-era monuments the new governments blew up or tore down, the positive legacies of socialism were still everywhere in Bulgaria, especially on TV. Bulgaria once had a thriving domestic film industry, one that was crushed after 1989 by an onslaught of Western programs and Latin American *tele-*

novelas. At some point after 2001, however, Bulgarian National Television started to reshow these old movies, films about Bulgaria made by Bulgarians. They were a part of the country's history, and despite the fact that they were produced during an era of strict ideological control and censorship, they tried their best to reflect what everyday life had been like for people under communism. For young people like my nephew born around 1989, the message was pretty clear: not everything about communism had been bad.

This point struck home when I was recently rewatching my favorite Bulgarian film, *Orkestar bez ime* (The orchestra with no name, or The nameless band). The movie is about a couple of friends who form a band, hoping to get rich and famous by playing on the Bulgarian Black Sea coast for Western tourists. Released in January 1982, almost eight years before the Changes, the movie pokes fun at the Communist regime in a lighthearted (and therefore perhaps nonthreatening) way. It is a story about friendship and betrayal and what it meant to be a young person during socialism, full of crazy dreams and hilarious mishaps. Despite its implicit criticisms of the Communist regime, the film won several prizes from the Union of Bulgarian Film Artists in 1982 and has become one of the all-time cult favorites in Bulgaria. Young Bulgarians will inevitably see this film and will make their own assessments of the past. The future of countries like Bulgaria is in the hands of its youth, young people like my nephew who have been raised entirely under a capitalist system but are constantly reminded that there was once another way, a dream for a more just society.

Understanding this process of remembering socialism in Eastern Europe is key to comprehending what the future holds in store for different postcommunist countries. Studying the quotidian, the forgotten stories of ordinary people who lived more or less ordinary lives, can help make sense of this longing for a totalitarian past. It may also help us make sense of the things that we take for granted in our daily lives. What would we do if we experienced the same magnitude of political and economic upheaval as men and women in the former Eastern Bloc did? After all, the Soviet Union was once a superpower too, and no one saw its demise coming until it was already gone.

The short collection of stories in this book has captured the experiences of but a handful of people whose paths at one point or another crossed my own. Hearing stories like these can help us make sense of broader geopolitical trends, but I also believe that they are important in their own right. The collapse of communism was an unprecedented historical event involving the implosion of a global empire that controlled enough nuclear weapons to destroy the planet, an empire that defined human history for the entire twentieth century. The reverberations of this collapse and the lingering appeal of Marxist-Leninist ideas are still with us, and it is unlikely that they will disappear anytime soon. The arch of history is long, much longer than any one individual life. But it is the small histories of these individual lives that ultimately inform the grand narratives of historical progress. Paying attention to the quotidian, to the way that ordinary life goes on despite social and political upheaval, can remind us of our common humanity. And like Ani's unfulfilled wish at the end of "Comrades," it just may be that, on the most basic level, we really are drugari to each other after all.

Notes

1. Pew Research Center, "The Pulse of Europe 2009: 20 Years After the Fall of the Berlin Wall. End of Communism Cheered But Now with More Reservations," *Pew Global Attitudes Project* (November 2, 2009) 114, Q20a, http://pewglobal.org/reports/display.php?ReportID=267.
2. Ibid., 14.
3. Ibid., 40.
4. Ibid., 32.
5. Vesselin Zhelev, "Ally Threatens to Abandon Borisov over Praise of Zhivkov," WAZ EUObserver (November 17, 2010), http://waz.euobserver.com/887/31285.
6. Joakim Ekman and Jonas Linde, "Communist Nostalgia and the Consolidation of Democracy in Central and Eastern Europe," *Journal of Communist Studies and Transition Politics* 21, no. 3 (September 2005): 354–74.
7. Ibid., 359–60.
8. Ibid., 369–70.
9. *Osennii krizis 1998 goda: possiiskoie obchtchestvo do i posle*, PNISiNP, Rosspen, Moscow, 1998, cited in Jean-Marie Chauvier, "Russia: Nostalgic for the Soviet Era," *Le Monde Diplomatique* (March 2004), http://mondediplo.com/2004/03/11russia.
10. Pew Research Center, "The Pulse of Europe 2009: 20 Years after the Fall of the Berlin Wall. End of Communism Cheered But Now with More Reservations," 55.
11. 2007 Forsa Institute Data cited in Kate Connelly, "Germans Hanker After Barrier," *The Guardian*, November 8, 2007, http://www.guardian.co.uk/world/2007/nov/08/germany.international.

12. Gfk Piackutató data cited in Hungary Around the Clock, "Poll Shows Majority of Hungarians Feel Life Was Better under Communism," May 21, 2008, www .politics.hu, http://www.politics.hu/20080521/poll-shows-majority-of-hungar ians-feel-life-was-better-under-communism.

13. Pew Research Center, "The Pulse of Europe 2009," 23.

14. Ibid., 25.

15. Ibid., 28.

16. Marian Adnanes, "Social Transaction and Anomie among Post-Socialist Bulgarian Youth," *Young* 15, no. 1 (2007): 49–69.

17. See Kristen Ghodsee, "Red Nostalgia? Communism, Women's Emancipation, and Economic Transformation in Bulgaria," *L'Homme: Zeitschrift für Feministische Geschichtswissenschaft* 15, no. 1 (2004): 23–36; and Eckman and Linde, "Communist Nostalgia." For an excellent study on the general nature of nostalgia, see Svetlana Boym, *The Future of Nostalgia* (New York: Basic Books, 2002).

18. David Stark and Laszlo Bruszt, *Postsocialist Pathways: Transforming Politics and Property in East Central Europe* (Cambridge: Cambridge University Press, 1998).

19. I have detailed this process at length in my two previous books. See Kristen Ghodsee, *The Red Riviera: Gender, Tourism, and Postsocialism on the Black Sea* (Durham: Duke University Press, 2005) and Kristen Ghodsee, *Muslim Lives in Eastern Europe: Gender, Ethnicity, and the Transformation of Islam in Postsocialist Bulgaria* (Princeton: Princeton University Press, 2010).

20. Sofia News Agency, "Bulgarian PM Implicates Power Utilities, Political Lobbyists in 'Robbery,' " April 8, 2010, http://www.novinite.com/view_news.php?id =115019.

21. Sofia News Agency, "Bulgaria's Ruling Majority Implodes over Proposed Banking Regulation," June 1, 2010, http://www.novinite.com/view_news.php?id =116744.

22. See, for instance, Janine R. Wedel, *Collision and Collusion: The Strange Case of Western Aid to Eastern Europe* (New York, Palgrave, 2001).

23. Maria Todorova, "Daring to Remember Bulgaria, Pre-1989," *Guardian.co.uk*, November 9, 2009, http://www.guardian.co.uk/commentisfree/2009/nov/ 09/1989-communism-bulgaria.

24. Natalya Baranskaya, *A Week Like Any Other: Novellas and Stories* (Seattle: Seal Press, 1993).

TIMELINE OF TWENTIETH-CENTURY COMMUNISM

1917	Lenin's Bolsheviks seize power in Russia and set up the first Soviet state, marking the establishment of communism in Europe.
1918–1919	The German Revolution includes multiple Communist revolts, and the founding of the short-lived Bavarian Soviet Republic.
1918–1920	Western countries send aid to counterrevolutionary forces in Russia, but the Red Army is ultimately victorious.
1919	Lenin establishes the Communist International (Comintern) to support an international Communist revolution. Over the next several years, Ukraine, the Caucasus, and Central Asia become incorporated into the Union of Soviet Socialist Republics.
1921	Mongolia becomes a Communist country.
1924	Lenin dies. Stalin, Trotsky, and Bukharin jointly rule the USSR, until Stalin consolidates power in 1927.
1928	In order to enable the Soviet Union to "catch and overtake" the Western capitalist world, Stalin introduced the First Five-Year Plan, a program of rapid industrialization and forced collectivization of agriculture.
1929	The stock market crashes in the United States and the Great Depression begins.
1933	The United States has formal diplomatic ties with the USSR for the first time.

1934	The Soviet Union joins the League of Nations (until its expulsion in 1939).
1939	Ribbentrop-Molotov Pact (a nonaggression treaty) is signed between the USSR and Germany. Germany and Russia invade Poland. World War II begins.
1940	The Baltic States: Latvia, Lithuania, and Estonia, are annexed into the USSR.
1941	Germany invades the USSR. Japan attacks Pearl Harbor. The United States enters the war. The Soviet Union is an allied country.
1943	The Socialist Federal Republic of Yugoslavia becomes a Communist country.
1944	There is a Communist coup in Bulgaria. There are increasing conflicts between the British and procommunist forces in Greece. Poland becomes a Communist country.
1945	Germany surrenders. World War II ends. Romania becomes a Communist country.
1946	Churchill says that an "Iron Curtain" has fallen across Europe. Bulgaria becomes a Communist country. Albania becomes a Communist country.
1947	The US Congress grants $400 million in aid to put down Communist revolutions in Greece and Turkey. Poland becomes a Communist country. The Soviet-dominated Organization of Communist Parties (Cominform, or Information Bureau of the Communist and Workers' Parties) is founded.
1948	Czechoslovakia becomes a Communist country. North Korea becomes a Communist country. Stalin and Tito split over the road to Socialism.
1949	Germany is divided and East Germany becomes a Communist country. Hungary becomes a Communist country. China becomes a Communist country; one-fourth of the world's population is now in the "red" camp. The USSR successfully tests its first atomic bomb and becomes the world's second nuclear power. The North Atlantic Treaty Organization (NATO) is formed to prevent further Communist expansion in Europe (Belgium, Canada, Denmark, France, Iceland, Italy, Luxembourg, the Netherlands, Norway, Portugal, the United Kingdom, and the United States).

1950	China and the USSR sign the Sino-Soviet Pact (a bilateral defense commitment). North Korea crosses the thirty-eighth parallel and the Korean War begins.
1952	Gamal Abdul Nasser leads a leftist, nationalist coup in Egypt.
1953	The Korean War ends (North Korea stays Communist). Socialist-leaning government gains power in Iran, but a US-backed coup installs the Shah. Stalin dies. Khrushchev becomes leader of the USSR and consolidates power by 1955.
1954	US-backed coup overthrows an elected leftist government in Guatemala. The Communist Party is outlawed in the United States. Communist North Vietnam is established. Communist insurgency in the Philippines is defeated. Egypt becomes an important Soviet ally.
1955	The Warsaw Pact is signed: this is the Communist counterpart to NATO and includes East Germany, Czechoslovakia, Poland, Hungary, Romania, Albania, Bulgaria, and the Soviet Union. Soviet aid to Syria begins; Syria becomes an ally of the USSR.
1956	Khrushchev gives his "secret speech" prompting de-Stalinization in the USSR. Communist-leaning government in Egypt nationalizes the Suez Canal. Hungarian uprising against the USSR; Russia invades Hungary to crush revolt. France and UK declare war on Egypt. Khrushchev tells the West, "We will bury you!"
1957	Soviet Union launches Sputnik, the first satellite in space. Soviet Union launches Sputnik 2, with the first living creature in space (a dog).
1958	The United States establishes NASA. There is a Soviet-backed coup in Iraq; Iraq becomes a Soviet ally.
1959	Cuba becomes a Communist country. Castro expropriates all American businesses in Cuba. Soviet spacecraft reaches the moon, but crashes there.
1960	Communist insurgency in Laos begins.
1961	Yuri Gagarin is the first man in space. Kennedy authorizes advisors to South Vietnam. Kennedy pledges to put a man on the moon before the end of decade. The Berlin Wall is built. The Soviet Union successfully tests the most powerful nuclear weapon thus far. The United States invades Cuba but fails to oust Castro during the Bay of Pigs.

1962	John Glenn is the first American in space. The Cuban Missile Crisis brings the world to the brink of nuclear annihilation.
1963	Kennedy is assassinated. Valentina Tereshkova becomes the first woman in space.
1964	Congo becomes a Communist country. Coup installs a leftist government in Brazil. The Vietnam War begins. Brezhnev replaces Khrushchev as the leader of the USSR.
1965	US Marines land in Vietnam. US troops invade the Dominican Republic to prevent Communist government. Communist coup fails in Indonesia.
1966	A Soviet spacecraft makes a landing on the moon. Another one crashes onto the surface of the planet Venus.
1967	South Yemen becomes a Communist country.
1968	The Brezhnev Doctrine justifies invasion of states attempting to leave the Warsaw Pact. Prague Spring reforms occur: "Socialism with a Human Face." The Red Army invades Czechoslovakia.
1969	The United States bombs Cambodia to prevent communism. Americans land on the moon. Coup in Libya brings the country into the Soviet camp.
1970	US troops invade Cambodia. Socialist government is democratically elected in Chile. US report shows eighty-eight countries with communist-type parties or movements. US congressional "Theory and Practice of Communism" hearings begin.
1973	US-backed coup ousts democratically elected Socialist leader of Chile.
1974	Ethiopia becomes a Communist country.
1975	The United States pulls out of Cambodia, Cambodia becomes a Communist country. Saigon falls to North Vietnamese troops. Mozambique becomes a Communist country.
1976	Vietnam (North and South) becomes a Communist country. Angola becomes a Communist country.
1978	Afghanistan becomes a Communist country.

1979	Nicaragua becomes a Communist country. Civil war begins in El Salvador. The USSR invades Afghanistan to support Communist government.
1980	Ronald Reagan elected president of the United States. Solidarity, a noncommunist trade union, is founded in Poland.
1981	Martial law is declared in Poland to crush the Solidarity trade union.
1983	The United States invades Grenada to prevent communism.
1985	Gorbachev becomes the leader of the USSR.
1986	The Chernobyl nuclear accident occurs in the Ukraine.
1987	Perestroika (restructuring) begins in the USSR.
1989	Tiananmen Square demonstrations occur in China. The Berlin Wall falls. Democratic revolutions occur across Eastern Europe without Soviet interference.
1990	Germany is reunified.
1991	The Soviet Union falls. The breakup of the USSR begins. Boris Yeltsin becomes the president of Russia. Yugoslav wars of independence begin.

FURTHER READING

Although there are only a handful of explicit citations in the book, this work is informed by a vast body of ethnographic literature on postsocialism produced by scholars in both North America and Europe. What follows below is a *very selected* list of books in English for those interested in learning more about the history of communism and the anthropology of postsocialism. I have arranged these texts alphabetically by author and by country. While by no means an exhaustive list, these books represent a small sample of the variety of English-language scholarship that has engaged with both the large and small questions in the field of transitology.

Selected General Histories of Communism

Pipes, Richard. *Communism: A History*. New York: Modern Library, 2003.

Priestland, David. *The Red Flag: A History of Communism*. New York: Grove Press, 2009.

Service, Robert. *Comrades! A World History of Communism*. Cambridge: Harvard University Press, 2007.

Selected General Books on Postsocialism

Berdahl, Daphne, Matti Bunzl, and Martha Lampland, eds. *Altering States: Ethnographies of Transition in Eastern Europe and the Former Soviet Union*. Ann Arbor: University of Michigan Press, 2000.

Burawoy, Michael, and Katherine Verdery, eds. *Uncertain Transition: Ethnographies of Change in the Postsocialist World*. New York: Rowman and Littlefield, 1999.

Gal, Susan, and Gail Kligman, eds. *Reproducing Gender: Politics, Publics, and Everyday Life After Socialism*. Princeton: Princeton University Press, 2000.

Hann, Chris M. *Not the Horse We Wanted! Postsocialism, Neoliberalism, and Eurasia.* Münster: LIT, 2006.

Humphrey, Caroline, and Katherine Verdery. *Property in Question: Value Transformation in the Global Economy.* New York: Berg Press, 2004.

Mandel, Ruth, and Caroline Humphrey, eds. *Markets and Moralities: Ethnographies of Postsocialism.* New York: Berg, 2002.

Todorova, Maria. *Remembering Communism: Genres of Representation.* New York: Social Science Research Council, 2010.

Todorova, Maria, and Zsuzsa Gille. *Postcommunist Nostalgia.* New York: Berghahn Books, 2010.

Verdery, Katherine. *What Was Socialism, and What Comes Next?* Princeton: Princeton University Press, 1996.

Albania

De Waal, Clarissa. *Albania Today: A Portrait of Post-Communist Turbulence.* London: I. B. Tauris, 2005.

Pajo, Erind. *International Migration, Social Demotion, and Imagined Advancement: An Ethnography of Socioglobal Mobility.* New York: Springer, 2007.

Stahl, Johannes. *Rent from the Land: A Political Ecology of Postsocialist Rural Transformation.* New York: Anthem Press, 2010.

Young, Antonia. *Women Who Become Men: Albanian Sworn Virgins.* New York and Oxford: Berg, 2011.

Bulgaria

Buchanan, Dana. *Balkan Popular Culture and the Ottoman Ecumene: Music, Image, and Regional Political Discourse.* Lanham: The Scarecrow Press, 2007.

———. *Performing Democracy: Bulgarian Music and Musicians in Transition.* Chicago: University of Chicago Press, 2006.

Cellarius, Barbara. *In the Land of Orpheus: Rural Livelihoods and Nature Conservation in Postsocialist Bulgaria.* Madison: University of Wisconsin Press, 2004.

Creed, Gerald. *Domesticating Revolution: From Socialist Reform to Ambivalent Transition in a Bulgarian Village.* University Park: Penn State University Press, 1998.

Ghodsee, Kristen. *Muslim Lives in Eastern Europe: Gender, Ethnicity, and the Transformation of Islam in Postsocialist Bulgaria.* Princeton: Princeton University Press, 2010.

———. *The Red Riviera: Gender, Tourism, and Postsocialism on the Black Sea.* Durham: Duke University Press, 2005.

Kaneff, Deema. *Who Owns the Past? The Politics of Time in a 'Model' Bulgarian Village.* New York: Berghahn Books, 2006.

Silverman, Carol. *Romani Routes: Cultural Politics and Balkan Music in Diaspora.* Oxford: Oxford University Press, 2010.

The Czech Republic and Slovakia (formerly Czechoslovakia)

Dery, Dominka. *The Twelve Little Cakes: Memoir of a Prague Childhood.* New York: Riverhead Books, 2004.

Epstein, Helen. *Where She Came From: A Daughter's Search for Her Mother's History.* New York: Plume Books, 1997.

Hall, Timothy McCajor, and Rosie Read. *Changes in the Heart of Europe: Recent Ethnographies of Czechs, Slovaks, Roma, and Sorbs.* Stutgart: Ibidem-verlag, 2006.

Hoffman, Eva. *Exit into History: A Journey through the New Eastern Europe.* New York: Penguin Books, 1993.

Holy, Ladislav. *The Little Czech and the Great Czech Nation: National Identity and the Post-Communist Social Transformation.* Cambridge: Cambridge University Press, 1996.

Weiner, Elaine. *Market Dreams: Gender, Class, and Capitalism in the Czech Republic.* Ann Arbor: University of Michigan Press, 2007.

German Democratic Republic

Berdahl, Daphne. *On the Social Life of Postsocialism: Memory, Consumption, Germany.* Bloomington: Indiana University Press, 2009.

———. *Where the World Ended: Re-Unification and Identity in the German Borderland.* Berkeley: University of California Press, 1999.

Borneman, John. *Belonging in the Two Berlins: Kin, State, Nation.* Cambridge: Cambridge University Press, 1992.

———. *Settling Accounts: Violence, Justice, and Accountability in Postsocialist Europe.* Princeton: Princeton University Press, 1997.

Hungary

Fodor, Eva. *Working Difference: Women's Working Lives in Hungary and Austria, 1945–1995.* Durham: Duke University Press, 2003.

Gille, Zsuzsa. *From the Cult of Waste to the Trash Heap of History: The Politics of Waste in Socialist and Postsocialist Hungary.* Bloomington: Indiana University Press, 2007.

Haney, Lynne. *Inventing the Needy: Gender and the Politics of Welfare in Hungary.* Berkeley: University of California Press, 2002.

Harper, Krista. *Wild Capitalism: Environmental Activism and Postsocialist Political Ecology in Hungary.* Boulder: Columbia University Press, 2006.

Lampland, Martha. *The Object of Labor: Commodification in Socialist Hungary.* Chicago: University of Chicago Press, 1995.

Poland

Buchowski, Michal. *Reluctant Capitalists: Class and Culture in a Local Community in Western Poland*. Berlin: Centre Marc Bloch, 1997.

Dunn, Elizabeth C. *Privatizing Poland: Baby Food, Big Business, and the Remaking of Labor*. Ithaca: Cornell University Press, 2006.

Ost, David. *The Defeat of Solidarity: Anger and Politics in Postcommunist Europe*. Ithaca: Cornell University Press, 2005.

———. *Solidarity and the Politics of Anti-Politics: Opposition and Reform in Poland since 1968*. Philadelphia: Temple University Press, 1991.

Schneider, Deborah. *Being Goral: Identity Politics And Globalization in Postsocialist Poland*. Albany: State University of New York, 2006.

Romania

Kideckel, David. *The Solitude of Collectivism: Romanian Villagers to the Revolution and Beyond*. Ithaca: Cornell University Press, 1993.

Kligman, Gail. *The Politics of Duplicity: Controlling Reproduction in Ceausescu's Romania*. Los Angeles: University of California Press, 1998.

———. *The Wedding of the Dead: Ritual, Poetics, and Popular Culture in Transylvania*. Berkeley: University of California Press, 1990.

Verdery, Katherine. *National Ideology Under Socialism: Identity and Cultural Politics in Ceausescu's Romania*. Berkeley: University of California Press, 1991.

———. *The Political Lives of Dead Bodies: Reburial and Postsocialist Change*. New York: Columbia University Press, 1999.

———. *Transylvanian Villagers: Three Centuries of Political, Economic, and Ethnic Change*. Berkeley: University of California Press, 1983.

———. *The Vanishing Hectare: Property and Value in Postsocialist Transylvania*. Ithaca: Cornell University Press, 2003.

Russia and the Former Soviet Union

Adams, Laura. *The Spectacular State: Culture and National Identity in Uzbekistan*. Durham: Duke University Press, 2010.

Allina-Pisano, Jessica. *The Post-Soviet Potemkin Village: Politics and Property Rights in the Black Earth*. Cambridge: Cambridge University Press, 2007.

Balzer, Marjorie Mandelstam. *The Tenacity of Ethnicity: A Siberian Saga in Global Perspective*. Princeton: Princeton University Press, 1999.

Bilaniuk, Laada. *Contested Tongues: Language Politics and Cultural Correction in Ukraine*. Ithaca: Cornell University Press, 2006.

Caldwell, Melissa. *Not by Bread Alone: Social Support in the New Russia*. Berkeley: University of California Press, 2004.

Crate, Susan. *Cows, Kin, and Globalization: An Ethnography of Sustainability*. Lanham: AltaMira Press, 2006.

Fitzpatrick, Sheila, *Everyday Stalinism: Ordinary Life in Extraordinary Times*. Oxford: Oxford University Press, 2000.

Goluboff, Sascha. *Jewish Russians: Upheavals in a Moscow Synagogue*. Philadelphia: University of Pennsylvania Press, 2003.

Grant, Bruce. *The Captive and the Gift: Cultural Histories of Sovereignty in Russia and the Caucasus*. Ithaca: Cornell University Press, 2009.

———. *In the Soviet House of Culture: A Century of Perestroikas*. Princeton: Princeton University Press, 1995.

Hemment, Julie. *Empowering Women in Russia*. Bloomington: Indiana University Press, 2007.

Humphrey, Caroline. *Marx Went Away—but Karl Stayed Behind*. Ann Arbor: University of Michigan Press, 1999.

———. *The Unmaking of Soviet Life: Everyday Economies After Socialism*. Ithaca: Cornell University Press, 2002.

Khazanov. Anatoly. *After the USSR: Ethnicity, Nationalism, and Politics in the Commonwealth of Independent States*. Madison: University of Wisconsin Press, 1996.

Ledeneva, Alena V. *How Russia Really Works: The Informal Practices that Shaped Post-Soviet Politics and Business*. Ithaca: Cornell University Press, 2006.

———. *Russia's Economy of Favours: Blat, Networking and Informal Exchange*. Cambridge University Press, 1998.

Lemon, Alaina. *Between Two Fires: Gypsy Performance and Romani Memory from Pushkin to Postsocialism*. Durham: Duke University Press, 2001.

Lindquist, Galina. *Conjuring Hope: Magic and Healing In Contemporary Russia*. New York: Berghahn Books, 2005.

Oushakine, Serguei. *The Patriotism of Despair: Nation, War, and Loss in Russia*. Ithaca: Cornell University Press, 2009.

Patico, Jennifer. *Consumption and Social Change in a Post-Soviet Middle Class*. Stanford: Stanford University Press, 2008.

Paxson, Margaret. *Solovyovo: The Story of Memory in a Russian Village*. Washington, D.C.: Woodrow Wilson Center Press, 2005.

Pelkmans, Mathijs. *Defending the Border: Identity, Religion, And Modernity in the Republic of Georgia*. Ithaca: Cornell University Press, 2006.

Pesmen, Dale. *Russia and Soul: An Exploration*. Ithaca: Cornell University Press, 2000.

Phillips, Sarah. *Women's Social Activism in the New Ukraine: Development and the Politics of Differentiation*. Bloomington: Indiana University Press, 2008.

Rausing, Sigrid. *History, Memory, and Identity in Post-Soviet Estonia: The End of a Collective Farm*. Oxford: Oxford University Press, 2004.

Reis, Nancy. *Russian Talk: Culture and Conversation during Perestroika*. Ithaca: Cornell University Press, 1997.

Richardson, Tanya. *Kaleidoscopic Odessa: History and Place in Contemporary Ukraine*. Toronto: University of Toronto Press, 2008.

Rivkin-Fish, Michele. *Women's Health in Post-Soviet Russia: The Politics of Intervention*. Bloomington: Indiana University Press, 2005.

Rogers, Douglas. *The Old Faith in the Russian Land: A Historical Ethnography of Ethics in the Urals*. Ithaca: Cornell University Press, 2009.

Shevchenko, Olga. *Crisis and the Everyday in Postsocialist Moscow*. Bloomington: Indiana University Press, 2008.

Ssorin-Chaikov, Nikolai. *The Social Life of the State in Subarctic Siberia*. Stanford: Stanford University Press, 2003.

Tishkov, Valery. *Chechnya: Life in a War-Torn Society*. Berkeley: University of California Press, 2004.

Uehling, Greta. *Beyond Memory: The Crimean Tatars' Deportation and Return*. New York: Palgrave Macmillan, 2004.

Vitebsky, Piers. *The Reindeer People: Living With Animals and Spirits in Siberia*. New York: Mariner Books, 2006.

Volkov, Vadim. *Violent Entrepreneurs: The Use of Force in the Making of Russian Capitalism*. Ithaca: Cornell University Press, 2002.

Wanner, Catherine. *Communities of the Converted: Ukrainians and Global Evangelism*. Ithaca: Cornell University Press, 2007.

——. *Burden of Dreams: History and Identity in Post-Soviet Ukraine*. Philadelphia: Pennsylvania State University Press, 1998.

Willerslev, Rane. *Soul Hunters: Hunting, Animism, and Personhood among the Siberian Yukaghirs*. Berkeley: University of California Press, 2007.

Wolfe, Thomas C. *Governing Soviet Journalism: The Press and the Socialist Person after Stalin*. Bloomington: Indiana University Press, 2005.

Yurchak, Alexei. *Everything Was Forever, Until It Was No More: The Last Soviet Generation*. Princeton: Princeton University Press, 2005.

Yugoslavia (and successor states)

Bringa, Tone. *Being Muslim the Bosnia Way*. Princeton: Princeton University Press, 1995.

Drakulic, Slavenka. *Café Europa: Life After Communism*. New York: Penguin, 1999.

——. *How We Survived Communism and Even Laughed*. New York: W. W. Norton and Co., 1993.

Kristen Ghodsee is John S. Osterweis Associate Professor of Gender
and Women's Studies at Bowdoin College.

Library of Congress Cataloging-in-Publication Data
Ghodsee, Kristen Rogheh
Lost in transition : ethnographies of everyday life after communism /
Kristen Ghodsee.
p. cm.
ISBN 978-0-8223-5089-7 (cloth : alk. paper)
ISBN 978-0-8223-5102-3 (pbk. : alk. paper)
1. Post-communism—Europe, Eastern. 2. Europe, Eastern—Social life
and customs. 3. Europe, Eastern—Social conditions. I. Title.
HN380.7.A8G48 2011
306.0947'09049—dc22   2011010760